The CYBERethics READER

Nancy E. Willard

The McGraw-Hill Companies, Inc.
New York St. Louis San Francisco Auckland Bogotá
Caracas Lisbon London Madrid Mexico City Milan
Montreal New Delhi San Juan Singapore Tokyo Toronto

McGraw-Hill

*A Division of The **McGraw·Hill** Companies*

The Cyberethics Reader

1 2 3 4 5 6 7 8 9 0   S E M S E M   9 0 9 8 7

ISBN 0-07-070318-3

Sponsoring editor: Rhonda Sands
Associate editor: Courtney Attwood
Editorial assistant: Kyle Thomes
Production supervisor: Natalie Durbin
Project manager/text designer: Cecelia G. Morales
Cover designer: Elizabeth Williamson
Copyeditor: Sylvia Townsend
Compositor: Cecelia G. Morales
Printer and binder: Quebecor Printing Semline, Inc.

Library of Congress Card Catalog No. 96-77645

http://www.mhcollege.com

This book is dedicated to my son, Jordan, and my daughter, Darlin,
and to the future world they will inherit.

Contents

Preface

"We are doing a fine job at teaching our students to use the Internet. But we need to focus on educating them to be good cyberspace citizens."

*t*his was the comment recently made by a university professor. Her concern is shared by others:

+ Employers and government agencies who are concerned about employee use of the Internet.
+ Internet providers who are weary of hassles with users who abuse system privileges.
+ Parents who want their children to use the Internet safely and effectively.
+ And everyday Net users who just don't know what the standards are in this new and ever-changing environment.

Bookstores continue to clear space for the explosive growth of Internet "how to" books, some with brief sections on netiquette issues. Netiquette guides are available on the Internet itself. This book offers a succinct yet comprehensive guide to cyberethics.

Some Internet issues, such as copyright law and free speech, are complicated and worthy of full academic treatises, which this book does not claim to be. But, as complicated as these issues are, this book offers simple guidelines that individuals can follow to be good cyberspace citizens.

The Cyberethics Reader supports course work in all disciplines, ranging from education to business. A Web site has been established to provide links to more extensive materials that will facilitate a deeper analysis of current ethics issues. Visit the site at http://mgh.willamette.edu/mgh/. In addition, this book can be used to support company or government agency training sessions on using the Internet.

Obviously, it is not possible to write a book without the help of family and friends who are willing to provide input and suggestions and to review the work while it was in progress. The family, friends, and reviewers who have helped along the way are: Alice Schreiber, Miles Willard, David Willard,

Janice Willard Nilsson, John Williamson, Nicole Douglas, Paul O'Driscoll, Dorothy Rogers, David Klindt, Bob Block, Bill Hoyt, Tom Lindly, Henry Kaplan, Aaron Munter, Judy Hallman, Jerry Taylor, Stephanie Chenault (College of Charleston), Dr. Timothy Gottleber (North Lake College), Daris Howard (Ricks College), Barbara Johnson (University of Connecticut), and LoriLee Sadler (DePaul University).

Nancy E. Willard
July 27, 1996

Introduction

if you understand the history and basic structure of the Internet you will also understand why it's so important that, as a society, we stress the need for ethics and personal responsibility.

The underlying technology of the Internet was developed by the United States military to facilitate communications between the computers and computer networks of the military, defense contractors, and university laboratories that were conducting defense-related research. The Findings of Fact set forth in the recent U.S. District Court decision in the case related to the Computer Decency Act described the key aspects of the organizational structure of the Internet:[1]

> "The network was designed to be a decentralized, self-maintaining series of redundant links, capable of rapidly transmitting communications without direct human involvement or control, and with the automatic ability to reroute communications if one or more individual links were damaged or otherwise unavailable. Among other goals, this redundant system of linked computers was designed to allow vital research and communications to continue even if portions of the network were damaged, say, in a war." (Finding 6)

> "No single entity—academic, corporate, governmental or non-profit— administers the Internet. It exists and functions as a result of the fact that hundreds of thousands of separate operators of computers and computer network independantly decided to use common data transfer protocols to exchange communications and information with other computers. . . . There is no centralized storage location, control point, or communications channel for the Internet, and it would not be technically feasible for a single entity to control all of the information conveyed on the Internet. " (Finding 11)

> "The Internet is therefore a unique and wholly new medium of worldwide human communication." (Finding 81)

---

[1] *ACLU v. Janet Reno,* U.S. District Court for the Eastern District of Pennsylvania, Case No. 93-693. June 11, 1996.

While national laws, international treaties and technological controls will continue play a role in governing activities on the Internet, it's clear that we've created a structure where traditional methods of government won't be wholly successful. We've created an electronic anarchy. Interestingly, there are two distinctly different definitions of anarchy:[2]

1. A utopian society governed through the cooperative and voluntary association of individuals and groups.
2. Political and social disorder, confusion, and chaos.

Either result could presumably occur in an environment that has no ruler, and whether we ultimately end up with Utopia or chaos depends on what we do now. Some will argue that we need a traditional "authority" to maintain an ethical and moral society, but the current structure of the Internet suggests that the power of authority and external control will continue to dissipate as we move further into the information age.

The question, then, is *how to avoid disintegration into disorder and instead achieve Utopia.* We can strive to foster a global society where people function with a high degree of internalized, individual control based on strong ethical and moral principals; a society that functions effectively through cooperative, voluntary action. This is not a new concept—it's a continuation of the teachings of the world's spiritual leaders throughout the ages. It's just becoming more important as the world population grows. As the power of external control dissipates, it's all that we have to rely on for the future of our planet.

---

[2] *Anarchy* n. 1. a state of society without government or law. 2. political and social disorder due to the absence of covernmental control. 3. a theory that regards the absence of all direct or coercive government as a political ideal and that proposes the cooperative voluntary association of individuals and groups as the principal mode of organized society. 4. confusion; choas; disorder. *Random House Webster's College Dictionary.* 1992.

Just because you can, doesn't make it right

Whenever you are to do a thing, though it can never be known but to yourself, ask yourself how you would act were all the world looking at you and act accordingly.

Thomas Jefferson

*t*he Net is a new frontier that offers a kind of freedom not generally found in the "real world." It is an environment where there is not only greater freedom, but where the laws, rules, and social standards are not quite as clear, or perhaps not quite as enforceable, as we have come to expect in other areas of our lives. How will you choose to respond to this new level of freedom?

At one extreme, there are people who maintain that they should have the freedom and right to use the Net in whatever way they choose, without regard for the harm they may inflict upon others. These people place a high priority on their own individual freedom, often to the detriment of the rights of other individuals or the common good. What they fail to recognize is that individual freedom, unguided by social and ethical values, is nothing more than mob rule.

At the other extreme, some people in our society have significant misgivings about the freedom that the Net provides and would like to find ways to restrict that freedom through the imposition of external control—more rules and laws.

It would appear that neither of these approaches holds much promise. The successful operation of the Net will depend on those who hold a different philosophy:

People who value individual freedom, but recognize that individual freedom must be balanced by personal responsibility, respect for others, and concern for the common good.

In an environment where external control cannot be relied upon to restrict harmful behavior, the entire issue comes down to personal choice:

✦ Some people in our society have established an internal system of values that embraces a balance between individual freedom and responsibility to others and to the common good. These people act in accordance with their values, even when they are in an environment that allows them the freedom to do otherwise. They will do what is right, not what they can get away with.

✦ Other people have not internalized a set of values. They think primarily of themselves, not of others or of the common good. These people may behave appropriately when there is a good chance they will get into trouble if they don't. But when they enter an environment where there is less chance of getting caught, they tend to act without regard for others. They will do what they can get away with.

Your use of the Net will reflect who you are.

✦ Is individual freedom your guiding value?

✦ What value do you place on respect for the rights of others and on the common good?

✦ What happens when your individual rights are in conflict with someone else's rights? Should your individual freedom to flail your fist in the air end when your fist is in the proximity of another person's nose?

✦ How will you choose to act in an environment where there is more freedom, but less clarity about rules and social standards and when and how they will be enforced?

Those are real people out there

It is a terrible, an inexorable law that one cannot deny the humanity of another without diminishing one's own; in the face of one's victim, one sees oneself.

James Baldwin

Therefore all things whatsoever ye would that men should do to you, do ye even so to them.

Matthew 7:12

*W*hen you communicate electronically all you see are the words on a screen. You cannot see facial expressions or gestures. You cannot hear a tone of voice. All you have are the typed words in front of you.

Social scientists tell us that we tend to adjust our actions based on the responses of people around us. When you communicate electronically, it is much harder to assess the responses of other people. It's easy to forget that you are communicating with a real person—a person who has feelings very much like your own, feelings that can be hurt. Thus, people tend to feel free to say things on the Net that they would never say to a person face to face.

For this reason, the Golden Rule is every bit as important in Cyberspace as it is in the real world:

Treat others the way you would like to be treated.

Before you push the Send button, ask yourself two questions:

✦ Would I say this if the person were sitting in front of me?

✦ How would I feel if I, or someone I cared for, received this message?

speak responsibly

At the heart of the First Amendment lies the principle that each person should decide for himself and herself the ideas and beliefs deserving of expression, consideration, and adherence. Our political system and cultural life rest upon this ideal. Government action that stifles speech on account of its message, or that requires the utterance of a particular message favored by the Government, contravenes this essential right. Laws of this sort pose inherent risk that the Government seeks not to advance a legitimate regulatory goal, but to suppress unpopular ideas or information or manipulate the public debate through coercion rather than persuasion. These restrictions raise the specter that Government may effectively drive certain ideas or viewpoints from the marketplace.

Justice Anthony Kennedy

But the character of every act depends upon the circumstances in which it is done. . . . The most stringent protection of free speech would not protect a man in falsely shouting fire in a theater and causing a panic.

Justice Oliver Wendell Holmes[3]

*t*he business of the Net is speech—collecting and disseminating information. Therefore, issues relating to freedom of speech on the Net are of paramount importance to its users and providers.[4]

Traditionally, the U.S. courts have extended a much higher level of free speech protection to material disseminated in print than to material disseminated through the broadcast medium. There are two reasons for this:

1. People have a greater level of control regarding the material they choose to read as compared to the material that is broadcast into their homes.

---

[3] *Turner Broadcasting System, Inc. v. FCC,* 114 S. Ct. 2445 (1994). *Schenck vs. U.S.,* 249 U.S. 47 (1919).

[4] The following analysis of free speech is based on U.S. law, which is similar, but not identical, to the law of many of the industrialized nations. But the Net is a global system and standards for free speech differ throughout the world. It will be interesting to see how the global use of the Net will affect free speech standards throughout the world.

2. Fostering the broad dissemination of ideas is at the heart of the First Amendment and, ostensibly, more people have the ability to disseminate their ideas through print than through broadcast.

Unfortunately, the idealized expectation that the multitudes would be able to communicate freely through print media has been tempered by the economic reality that most marketplaces of mass speech are dominated by relatively few media sources. The Net has changed the picture. As Judge Dalzell eloquently states in the U.S District Court decision in the case related to the Computer Decency Act:[5]

> It is no exaggeration to conclude that the Internet has achieved, and continues to achieve the most participatory marketplace of mass speech that this country—and indeed the world—has yet seen. . . . Indeed the Government's asserted "failure" of the Internet rests upon the implicit premise that too much speech occurs in this medium, and that speech is too available to the participants. This is exactly the benefit of Internet communication, however. The Government, therefore, implicitly asks this court to limit both the amount of speech on the Internet and the availability of that speech. This argument is profoundly repugnant to First Amendment principles. . . . As the most participatory form of mass speech yet developed, the Internet deserves the highest protection from Government intrusion."

As clear as this statement of the importance of the protection of free speech on the Net is, it should also be equally clear that those who engage in irresponsible speech should not expect to be immune from the consequences of their speech just because they happen to be speaking through the Net. Much of the discussion in this book relates to speech that is irresponsible—speech that is either illegal or can cause damage to someone else.

The right of free speech is not absolute. Under the First Amendment, speech can be regulated if there is an overriding public interest involved, such as the need to prevent child pornography or transmission of obscene material. Speech that occurs in the course of a crime, such as transmitting information on how to break into computer systems, is likewise not protected.

In addition to possible criminal liability, irresponsible speech can lead to civil liability. Just because speech may be protected does not mean that you cannot be held liable for harm caused by irresponsible speech. Civil liability for irresponsible speech can arise in cases such as defamation, harassment, intentional infliction of emotional distress, violation of privacy, and violation of trade secrets. In civil litigation, the courts generally try to balance society's interest in free speech against the harm caused by the speech and the ability of the particular defendant to have prevented such harm.

---

[5] *ACLU v. Janet Reno*, U.S. District Court for the Eastern District of Pennsylvania, Case No. 93-693. June 11, 1996.

It is important to recognize that First Amendment restrictions are only against government action. Private Net providers have the right to run their service as they choose. Providers have no First Amendment obligation to provide access to all newsgroups. In fact, they most likely have an affirmative obligation to remove newsgroups from the system if they know that these newsgroups carry illegal material, such as child pornography. Providers have no obligation to allow users to post any material they want on their Web pages. They likely have an affirmative obligation to remove illegal or damaging material if they know of its existence. And they have no obligation to provide an account to anyone who uses that account in a way that the provider considers to be inappropriate, such as sending harassing or junk e-mail.

Companies that have established Internet access to serve a company purpose have the right to determine what speech is, and is not, in furtherance of the company purpose. Government employees, including employees of educational institutions, do not have the right to use their system to communicate in whatever way they choose. Free speech rights of government employees are limited when they are acting in that capacity. Communicating through a government system would be considered acting in the capacity of a government employee. Students who are using a system established by an educational institution also have limited free speech rights. While institutions may not engage in viewpoint discrimination, they are within their rights to impose restrictions on speech for educationally-related purposes.[6] Any user of a restricted system can gain more expansive free speech rights by establishing a personal account through a private provider.

While individuals can always be held criminally or civilly responsible for irresponsible speech, the potential liability of system providers for speech that is transmitted through or presented on their system is not entirely clear. Under certain circumstances, entities that disseminate the speech of others can be held responsible for damage caused by that speech. Traditional legal analysis in cases related to defamation has focused on whether the entity distributing the speech is a publisher or a distributor.[7]

A publisher, such as a newspaper, is in a position to exercise editorial control and can be held liable for the damaging speech within a publication, not only if the publisher has knowledge of its presence but also if it has acted with "reckless disregard." The same standard is likely to be applied to system providers, Web publishers, and discussion group moderators if they exercise a similar level of editorial control. By contrast, distributors, such as bookstores, do not generally exercise editorial control and can only be held liable if they have actual knowledge or a reason to know of the damaging speech. The extent to which a provider, publisher, or moderator actually exercises editorial

---

[6] *Hazelwood School District v. Kuhlmeier*, 484 U.S. 260 (1988).

[7] These cases are decided under state law, which can vary from state to state.

control will vary, and therefore the potential liability will vary. But the potential for liability will always be present. Providers, publishers, and moderators must act responsibly if questions arise about the presence of damaging speech.

The Computer Decency Act attempted to impose criminal responsibility on system providers for indecent materials transmitted through or presented on their system. The court found that this was unacceptable because the term "indecent" is unconstitutionally vague and it is impossible for the system provider to review all such material. However, questions remain about the extent of potential liability of a system provider, Web publisher, and moderator for defamatory material, material that infringes upon the rights of the owner of a copyright, or other illegal material such as child pornography or obscene materials.

Why should the user be concerned about the potential liability of the system provider, publisher, or moderator? Because the higher the potential for liability, the more restrictive the provider, publisher, or moderator will likely be. The greater the lack of clarity, the more incentive there is to err on the side of restriction. In all likelihood, a balanced approach to the imposition of liability on providers, publishers, and moderators will emerge that will consider both the extent of editorial control and the actual knowledge of the defamatory, infringing, or illegal material.

We can also anticipate expanded interest in enhancing individual control over the material that is accessed through the Net or that comes to us through the Net. As important as the right to free speech is, we must also ensure our rights to be free *from* speech. We must have the ability to exercise control over the speech that we choose to be exposed to and to have our children exposed to through the Net. This includes not only material that we may find to be "indecent" according to our personal or family values, but also junk e-mail, and sites that pander to our children in the guise of online games.

It will take some time and more than a number of court cases to fully sort out free speech issues on the Net. While we should rejoice in the recent decision of the court on the Computer Decency Act, the decision does not provide license for those who would use the Net for irresponsible speech.

A college student posted a message to numerous newsgroups sharing confidential information about the alleged mistreatment of a young woman by her family and suggesting that the recipients place a telephone call to the family to complain about the mistreatment. The student's response to the objections to his action was: "You should be able to write what you want on the Internet, whether it's true or not."

In considering such a case, how would you balance the rights of free speech against the injury that can be caused by a person's exercise of free speech?

Look your best

The newest computer can merely compound, at speed, the oldest problem in relations between human beings, and in the end the communicator will be confronted with the old problem, of what to say and how to say it.

Edward R. Murrow

Unless one is a genius, it is best to aim at being intelligible.

Anthony Hope

*a*ppearance counts when you are communicating on the Net. You won't be judged by your physical appearance, your race, your hair color, or your age. But you will be judged by how you appear *in your writings*. You never know who might be *lurking*[8] or how looking your best could benefit you. People have received job offers, internship and study opportunities, book contracts, and even marriage proposals, all based on their appearance on the Net.

Here are some guidelines for looking your best when you send a personal e-mail message or post a message to a discussion group:[9]

✦ Be professional about what you say and how you say it. Know what you are talking about and be sure that what you are saying is correct to the best of your knowledge.

✦ Make sure that your message is clear and logical. Focus on one subject per message. Don't be long-winded.

✦ Use informative subject headings and present the most important information in your first several sentences. People frequently use a "triage" method when reading their e-mail. If the subject heading and first sentences do not immediately get their attention, they move on to the next

---

[8] *Lurking* is an Internet term for those people who are reading, but not posting, messages in a public forum.

[9] The terms *discussion group* or *group* will be used in this book to cover both mailing lists and newsgroups.

message. Try to present all the important information you wish to convey in the first screen. You can elaborate in the remainder of the message.

✦ Keep your paragraphs short and to the point. Include line breaks between your paragraphs. Reading e-mail on a computer screen can be a strain on the eyes. Short paragraphs with a space in between allow people to track through the message without getting lost.

✦ People tend to speed-read e-mail. You can assist their reading by making sure that your topic sentence is the first sentence in the paragraph and that the rest of the sentences in the paragraph relate to the topic sentence. If your message is long, use section headings to guide the reader.

✦ Add some color.[10] Using *asterisks* around words and phrases to emphasize a point, or a smiley :-) to indicate an emotion can make your post more interesting to read. You can also emphasize key points with bullets. But don't overdo it and PLEASE AVOID SHOUTING.[11]

✦ Use language that is straightforward and simple. Eschew obfuscatory verbosity.[12] Don't be redundant—avoid repeating yourself ;-).

✦ Be careful when using sarcasm and humor. In the absence of face-to-face communication, your joke could cause offense. It can also be very difficult for people from other cultures to understand "native" humor.

✦ Use a style and tone that is appropriate to the environment. While e-mail is generally more informal than a letter sent by snail mail, there are times when you will need to write in a more formal style. Your tone should always be friendly, but there is a difference between professionally friendly and overly casual.

✦ Be polite. Don't use offensive or sexist language.

✦ Cite all quotes, references, and sources. Make sure that your use of other people's work is within the fair use exemptions of copyright.[13]

✦ Demonstrate cultural sensitivity in your writing. Avoid using culturally-specific jargon and clichés or in any other way conveying the idea that your nation is the center of the world. Watch out for dates. Does the date 6/7/96 refer to June 7th or July 6th? It depends on your part of the world.

✦ Take the time to proofread your spelling, grammar, and punctuation.

✦ Always identify who you are. At the very least, include your name. If you are communicating in a subject area that relates to your employment position, include your title and address.

---

[10] Because e-mail is transmitted as plain text, Net communication conventions have been developed to convey more emphasis and meaning. A listing of the most common conventions is included in the Appendix "Net Communication Conventions," on page 97.

[11] Writing in all capitals is considered the online equivalent of shouting.

[12] Translation: Don't try to impress people with big words.

[13] See the chapters "Don't take without permission," on page 55, and "Credit the source," on page 53.

✦   Make sure you have addressed your message properly. There is nothing more embarrassing than sending a personal message to a discussion group.

———————

Look at some messages that make you think highly of the writer. Without considering the substance of the messages, what are some of the attributes of these particular messages that attract your attention and make you interested in reading them? Now look at some messages that make you think poorly of the writer and ones that you would quickly delete. What are some of the attributes of these messages that contribute to this perception or to your decision not to read the whole message?

Respect the privacy of others

I never said "I want to be alone."
I said, "I want to be left alone."
There's all the difference.

Greta Garbo

People have a right to privacy. Unfortunately, the ease with which personal information can be gathered, stored, and made available using technology is threatening this privacy. Resolving some of these privacy concerns will fall to the policymakers, but there are some ways that you can cultivate an appreciation and respect for privacy in your activities on the Net:

✦ Don't provide information about the personal details of another person's life or situation in a public or private message. Their personal information is their private business. Only they have the right to choose to disclose this information. Always keep in mind that you will have no control over the subsequent distribution of any message that you post that contains personal information about someone else.

✦ Treat what people say in their private messages to you with respect. Do not forward a message that was sent to you without the express permission of the author. It is generally considered acceptable to forward messages posted to a public discussion group; technically, however, such messages are still protected by copyright.[14]

✦ Don't read other people's e-mail or invade their personal storage space. This is not only a violation of their privacy, it is also a violation of unauthorized access laws.[15]

---

[14] See the section "Don't take without permission," on page 55.

[15] See the sections "Tread carefully," on page 21 and "Don't go where you don't belong," on page 35.

While companies generally have the right to access their employees' mail,[16] this does not mean that any employee has the right to snoop in other employees' e-mail or files. Hopefully, companies have clear policies regarding the circumstances under which an employee's e-mail or personal files can be accessed by others and the procedures to be followed.

✦ Be exceptionally careful with private company information, also called *trade secrets.* Your employer could suffer significant financial loss if company information were disclosed. As an employee, you have an obligation to protect your company's information. Be extremely careful about disclosing any company information through e-mail to a person outside your company. Hopefully, your employer has developed policies for e-mail and handling company information. But with or without such policies, don't join the unemployment line by failing to respect the privacy of company information.

Jane provided a rather scathing opinion of her supervisor in an e-mail message on her company account. Shortly thereafter, she was fired because of this message. Jane was under the mistaken belief that her e-mail was private, but, under current U.S. law, it is not.

How do you think employees' privacy and the interests of their company should be balanced?

---

[16] See the discussion on the privacy of employee e-mail in "Tread carefully," on page 21.

Remain cool under fire

The man who gets angry at the right things and with the right people, and in the right way and at the right time and for the right length of time is commended.

Aristotle

If someone offends you and you are in doubt as to whether it was intentional or not, do not resort to extreme measures; simply watch your chance and hit him with a brick.

Mark Twain

*i*t can happen to anyone. You read a message that pushes a "hot button" and you send off a fiery, impassioned retort, thereby igniting a *flame*[17] or offending someone you should not have offended.

Flaming is a long-standing tradition on the Net. It is sort of to be expected—we are, after all, human. However, the amount and style of flaming will vary from place to place. Controlled flaming has some good points. It can liven things up a bit or shake us out of our complacency. Sometimes it is important to respond with intensity—to make a point or to challenge something that you feel is really not acceptable. But there is a considerable difference between a thinking person who is responding with passion and a person who is going off half-cocked. If you are the former, others will likely respect the fact that your opinions are deeply held. If you are the latter, you are only doing damage to your reputation. Your messages will end up in *kill files*[18] or be deleted before they are read. And, like the boy who cried "wolf," you won't be taken seriously when you really are trying to be serious.

---

[17] *Flaming* is a netism that has a range of meanings from rude and obnoxious statements to impassioned statements.

[18] *Kill files* are a feature of newsreaders that allow the user to direct that files which meet certain criteria are automatically discarded.

Here are some tips on how to remain "passionately cool":

✦ Don't flame in the wrong places. In some groups, passionate statements and vigorous debate are acceptable; in other groups they are not.[19] Some individuals may understand and be forgiving if they receive a "hot" message; others may not be so forgiving.

✦ Challenge ideas or statements with which you disagree, but avoid engaging in personal attacks. That is the fastest way to lose the respect of your friends and colleagues.

✦ Being rude and obnoxious just for the sake of being rude and obnoxious is not OK.

✦ Don't flame often. A person who is always passionate is a person whose opinion will be discounted by others. Reserve your flames for the really important issues.

✦ Caution people that you are about to make a strong statement by writing, for example, "WARNING! FLAME ON!" at the beginning of your message. Making such a warning conveys an important message: "I am about to make an impassioned statement, but I am still in control and behaving responsibly."

✦ Keep your flame short and to the point. Make a clear, strong, logical case for your impassioned position. Then stop. You may want to go into longer explanations after you have posted your first message. Your subsequent explanations should always be more subdued.

✦ Never respond in an impassioned manner to something that is clearly "flame bait," a post that is intended to start a flame war.

✦ Never flame a *clueless newbie*[20] for making a mistake.

✦ If you are personally attacked, you are in a position to win or lose—and it's your call. If you respond with anger, you will lose big time. People will either believe your attacker or dismiss you both. You will emerge the big winner if you provide a reasoned, low-key response, maybe even one that includes a touch of humor to lighten things up or an apology if it is called for. If you can't make a reasoned response, keep your fingers off the keyboard until you have cooled down.

✦ Douse the flames quickly. While an impassioned exchange can liven up any discussion group, an extended argument between a small group of people is exceptionally boring to everyone else. State your case with passion, provide one or two follow-up messages of clarification or explanation, and then shut up.

---

[19] Also, see the chapter "Play by the rules of the house," on page 25.

[20] *Clueless newbie* is a netism for new users who have not yet found their way. See the following section, "We all begin as clueless newbies."

- ✦ If you find that people are often flaming you, take a good look at how you are expressing yourself. While not directly attacking people, you may be expressing yourself in a way that undercuts their sense of self-worth.
- ✦ Now, in the event that you have gone off half-cocked, the best thing to do is to send a quick apology and promise it will never happen again.

———

Find a series of messages that you consider to be a flame war. Look closely at the beginning messages in this series. Which message do you think started the flame war? Look at the message before this message. Did this writer trigger a flame war? If so, how? Think about how you might have written messages that conveyed the impassioned feelings of the participants without inciting a flame war.

We all begin as clueless newbies

If there is any kindness I can show, or any good thing I can do to any fellow being, let me do it now and not deter or neglect it, as I shall not pass this way again.

William Penn

Raise your hand if you have never made a mistake on the Net. Never sent a subscribe or unsubscribe message to a list, not the administrator. Never asked a question that was already in an *FAQ*.[21] Never sent a message to the wrong address. Never sent a message to a discussion group when you intended to send it to a person. Never misspelled a word. Never jumped at flame bait. Never made a fool of yourself.

Hands still in your lap? Welcome to the "Been There, Done That, Bought the T-shirt" Club.

Or you may still be a clueless newbie. Hopefully, you will be treated with respect when you make a mistake. Experienced users should try to remember how it feels when someone treats you rudely because you made a mistake.

Making mistakes is a normal part of learning and is to be expected. It's not a big deal. How can *you* help the clueless newbie who has made a mistake?

✦ Be forgiving. Demonstrate your good manners when addressing someone who has made a mistake. Don't violate the rules of netiquette by pointing out violations of netiquette in public. Flaming a newbie is just plain rude and inconsiderate.

✦ Send a polite message to the person, in private, pointing out the mistake and suggesting a more appropriate action. Providing a clueless newbie with a clue is a great way to lend a helping hand.

Who gave you your first clue? Were they helpful or hurtful?

---

[21] *FAQ* or *Frequently Asked Questions* is a document created for discussion groups that contains the answers to frequently asked questions.

Tread carefully

Look out how you use proud words.
When you let proud words go, it is not easy to call them back.
They wear long boots, hard boots.

Carl Sandburg

*d*o you remember Oliver North? He carefully deleted questionable messages from his e-mail box, only to find that they had all been saved by the conscientious system administrator who made regular back-ups of the system. Did you hear the story about the guy who was having an illicit affair with a coworker and sent her a very personal message—but accidentally cc'd it to the company distribution list?

Oops! You really ought to be careful. What you put on the Net can come back to haunt you.

✦ *Think if you post an outrageous statement, no one will ever find out?*
   Outrageous statements have a strong tendency to find their way to the place where you least want them to go—your teacher, your employer, your system administrator, your parent, your former best friend, and so forth.

✦ *Think you are in control?*
   When you send a message electronically, your words are in a form that allows them to be easily forwarded to another recipient. You have no control over where your message might end up. Sure, anyone who forwards your message without your permission will have violated your privacy, but, after the fact, there is little you can do except damage control.

✦ *Think you deleted your messages?*
   While you may have deleted them from your mailbox, your deletion will have no effect on what is retained in storage or is in someone else's mailbox.

✦ *Think encryption will keep your secrets secret?*
   The use of an encryption system may prevent the inadvertent disclosure of material that you wish to keep secret. But you can only be absolutely sure of keeping a secret if you are the only one who knows it. Can you

always trust that the recipient of your encrypted message will not forward it to others?

✦ *Think your personal files will always be private?*
Your personal files are accessible by any person with system privileges and may be invaded by a hacker if your system is not secure. While we hope that those with system privileges are scrupulous enough to keep their noses out of your files and that your system is secure, you can never be absolutely sure.[22]

If your account is on a school system, you have limited privacy rights. Most K–12 schools have acceptable use policies which provide that school officials have the right to inspect the contents of your private e-mail if they have a reasonable suspicion that you have violated a school rule or a law.[23] Many university acceptable use policies also allow for such inspection.

If you work for a company, you should be aware that your e-mail messages are not generally considered to be private.[24] The company established its e-mail system for use in business-related communications and your communications are considered company business. Unless your employer has made a special point of assuring the privacy of your electronic communications, they have the right to read any message you post.

If you are a public employee, which includes employees of public universities and schools, or an elected official, the contents of your personal e-mail files are maintained on a government system and are most likely considered part of the public record. This means that they could be requested by any citizen through the access-to-public-records process.

Thus the sage Net advice:

NEVER put anything in e-mail that you would not want to see on the evening news.

---

[22] A person who has invaded your personal space may have violated the law. See the chapter "Don't go where you don't belong," on page 35.

[23] As there are not yet any cases involving school inspection of a student's personal files, it is not clear what legal rights students may have to the privacy of their mail. But e-mail files are very similar to lockers—a place provided by the school where a student can keep personal material. School officials can perform routine maintenance on lockers and can make special inspections if they have a reasonable suspicion that they will find evidence that the student has violated a rule or the law. See *New Jersey v. T.L.O.*, 469 U.S. 325 (1985). The author has prepared an extensive legal analysis of K–12 acceptable use policies that is accessible through the website.

[24] The Electronic Communications Privacy Act, a U.S. federal law, provides some restrictions on employers in eavesdropping on or intercepting employee voice discussions, but is generally considered not to apply to e-mail. For an excellent discussion of electronic privacy, see Lance Rose, *Netlaw: Your Rights in the Online World* (Berkeley: McGraw-Hill, 1995).

When questions arose about some controversial appointments to a city commission, an intrepid reporter requested a copy of the e-mail records of the city councillors. The reporter discovered that several of the councillors had discussed the importance of these appointments as a way to ensure that their particular religious views would dominate the commission.

What have you put in e-mail that could come back to haunt you?

Play by the rules of the house

*i*t seems that no matter where you go in life, there are always rules or expectations for your behavior. On the Net, these rules fall into two categories: those that govern your use of your account and those that govern your activities in the various places you may trek.

Accepted Use Policies
The rules that govern the use of your account are generally called *acceptable use policies (AUPs)*. Virtually all providers have such policies.

Private Providers
Commercial providers tend to have the fewest restrictions on the use of their system. Policies will vary from provider to provider. It is important to note, however, that you have no inherent right to use your Internet account in whatever way you choose. Providers can set whatever policies they wish and can choose whether or not to provide you with an account.

Educational Systems

Your account on an education system, especially a K–12 system, may have more restrictive policies. Your educational institution is within its rights to restrict your use of this account to activities that have an educational purpose. For example:

◆ Educational institutions can place reasonable restrictions on your speech. Students do not "shed their constitutional rights to freedom of speech and expression at the schoolhouse gate"[25] or on the onramp to the school's connection to the information highway. But the Supreme Court has held that it is acceptable for school administrators to restrict students' speech if there is a valid educational reason for doing so.[26]

◆ Education systems generally prohibit use of the system for commercial or lobbying purposes.

◆ It is also within the authority of schools to restrict the kinds of sites that students can access through the Net.

Company and Government Systems

Employees who have an account through their place of business generally must use this account for business or agency purposes only. Companies have no obligation to use their resources to provide a public access service for their employees. Likewise, government agencies have no obligation to use taxpayer resources to provide a public access service for their employees. Companies and agencies also have legitimate concerns about the potential damage an employee can cause by making an outrageous statement using a company or agency account.

Employees should recognize that they can have no expectation of privacy on such accounts. Companies and agencies have the right to inspect e-mail. Additionally, it is within their authority to monitor how their employees are using the system and discipline them accordingly.

Rules on the Net

Special Conventions

The rules in the places you may trek while on the Net are generally unwritten ones—much like real-life social conventions and cultural norms. When you enter a new place on the Net, it's best to remain quiet at first to get a sense of the cultural norms before you jump into the conversation.

Generally, it is best not to disrupt the rules of the house of an established group or place on the Net. You may disagree with the rules, but it is more

---

[25] *Tinker v. Des Moines Independent Community School District*, 393 U.S. 503 (1969).

[26] In *Hazelwood School District v. Kuhlmeier*, 484 U.S. 260, 272-73 (1988), the Supreme Court stated: "We hold that educators do not offend the First Amendment by exercising editorial control over the style and content of student speech in school-sponsored expressive activities so long as their actions are reasonably related to legitimate pedagogical concerns."

respectful, and probably a better use of your time, to find a group or place with rules more to your liking.

In some discussion groups, a high priority may be placed on serious, intelligent discourse, while in other groups, trying to be serious will not be appreciated. There are also some places on the Net where there are no rules other than mob rule or "survival of the fittest."

Commercial Advertising

In many discussion groups there is a very strong cultural taboo against commercial advertising. There appear to be three basic cultural norms for advertising through discussion groups, which are listed on the next page.

✦ Groups where blatant advertising is expected and acceptable.

✦ Groups where blatant advertising is unacceptable, but where the subtle mention of the fact that you offer products or services, in the context of a message that makes a valuable contribution to the ongoing dialogue, would not be out of place. Sometimes the subtle mention would simply be the inclusion of your company name and slogan in your signature line.

✦ Groups where even the hint of a commercial interest is considered exceptionally inappropriate.

If you are using the Net for commercial activities, *please* be respectful of the desires of others not to have their mailboxes filled with junk e-mail.[27]

A government-affiliated research center announced that it was disciplining a significant number of employees who it had discovered were using the company Internet connection to visit sites containing pornography.

What is your opinion of the company's action?

If a computer system has been established by an educational institution, do you think that students should expect the institution to support their use of the system for entertainment purposes?

---

[27] Some suggestions on how to deal with the receipt of junk e-mail are found in the chapter "Speak up for your rights," on page 61.

Don't make noise

What is the measure of a worthwhile group? Why, it's Volume, Volume, Volume. Any group that has lots of noise in it must be good. Remember, the higher the volume of material in a group, the higher the percentage of useful, factual, and insightful articles you will find.

Emily Postnews Answers Your Questions on Netiquette

*t*he key in telecommunications transmissions is to maintain a good "signal-to-noise" ratio. "Signal" is the valuable data that is being transmitted. "Noise" is the static—the garbage—that gets in the way of the signal. An analogy can be made to the transmission of public or private messages on the Internet. Before you push the Send button, ask yourself: Are you transmitting a signal, something of value? Or are you just making noise?

When you send an electronic message you are taking someone's time. You have a responsibility to ensure that their time is not wasted. Remember, just about everyone on the Net is functioning on information overload. Please don't add to that overload.

✦ Make your posts short and to the point.

✦ Don't post to a group if a personal message will do.

✦ Make sure you stick to the topic of the particular group. If you aren't interested in the topic, go someplace else.

✦ When replying to a previous message, leave in enough original text so people know what you are responding to, but edit out anything not directly applicable to your reply.

✦ Do not commit one of the most unforgivable of Net offenses—copying the entire text of a long post and adding to the bottom the statement, "I agree," or, "Me, too."

✦ When posting a question to a group, request that responses be sent to you personally and not to the group. After you have received the responses, post an edited summary to the group. When responding to a question someone else has posted, send your response privately. You may, of course, post a reply to the group regarding topics being raised for discussion or questions in which there is likely to be general interest.

✦ Learn the proper procedures for administrative functions for a mailing list, especially for subscribing and unsubscribing. Always save the message that provides you with administrative information about the list so that you can refer to it for help. Don't post administrative questions to the group; contact the list administrator.

✦ Limit your signature line at the bottom to no longer than four or five lines.

✦ Don't send or forward long articles to a group. Provide a brief summary of the contents of the article and directions on how to find or receive it.

✦ Try not to ask stupid questions. Don't pose a question to an expert in the field or a discussion group without first having done enough research to know what you are asking about. If your group has a FAQ, check it before sending a question.

Respect resource limits

There's enough for our needs, but not for our greeds.

unknown

*t*here are limits to the resources of the Net. The Net is a network of net-works that have agreed to allow traffic to pass among them. The more traffic there is on the system, the more congested the network becomes, until, ulti-mately, the system can grind to a crawl or even a halt. This is just like a traffic jam on the freeway during rush hour—which is no fun for anyone. Your irre-sponsible actions could create "gridlock" on the information superhighway.

Your Net account has both local limits and network limits. The local limits are the amount of traffic your access provider can handle and the storage space on the system. The network limits are the traffic limits on the Net as a whole.

✦ Don't tie up the network with idle activities. Self-exploration is great, but there becomes a point where your are just wasting time and could be pre-venting others from accomplishing tasks that are important to them.[28]

✦ Download huge files only when absolutely necessary. The nice thing about the Internet is that it is not necessary to download everything. If you need more information from a particular source, you can always go back and find it.

✦ If you do need to download a large file, choose a time that is after normal business hours for both your local system and the remote system. Promptly remove large files from your system computer to your personal computer.

✦ Be responsible in your use of e-mail by following these guidelines:
   ✦ Check your e-mail regularly, preferably daily if you normally receive a lot of messages.
   ✦ Stay within any quotas your system may have for the storage of e-mail messages.

---

[28] See the chapter "Get a life," on page 65.

- ✦ Be selective when you subscribe to mailing lists. Don't put your system or yourself on overload with more messages than you can handle.
- ✦ If your mail is stored on the system computer, keep messages in your mailbox to a minimum. Download the ones you want to retain to your personal computer.
- ✦ If you have a high volume of mail and will be away from your mailbox for longer than a week, unsubscribe from your mailing lists temporarily so that your mail doesn't pile up.

✦ Don't tie up a dial-up connection to your access provider when it is not in use; other people could use this connection. When you log off, do so properly, so that the port is immediately available for other users.

✦ Don't send chain letters or unnecessary broadcast messages, or engage in *spamming*.[29] This creates network congestion, in addition to the indigestion of the people who have to deal with your unwanted messages.

---

[29] *Spamming* is sending unwanted and/or annoying messages to a large number of people. This concept of "spam" originated from a Monty Python script.

Ensure the integrity of the system

I am of the opinion that my life belongs to the community and as long as I live, it is my privilege to do for it whatever I can.

George Bernard Shaw

We abuse land because we regard it as a commodity belonging to us. When we see land as a community to which we belong, we may begin to use it with love and respect.

Aldo Leopold

*a*ll users have a responsibility to do their part to keep their local system and the Net secure. Your primary responsibility is for the security of your personal account. Because your account is a doorway into the system, you must keep that doorway secure. Take all reasonable precautions to prevent others from accessing your account.[30]

✦ Choose a good password, one that includes both letters and numbers. Don't choose a password that could easily be guessed by someone who knows you or who may have access to personal information about you. Change your password as requested by your access provider.

✦ Don't share your access code, account number, password, or other authentication that has been assigned to you.

✦ If you are asked to supply a password to enter a site on the Net, don't use your account password. Choose another password for these locations.

---

[30] In addition to protecting the system, you are protecting yourself by keeping your account secure. If you let a person use your account and they misuse it, you are the one who will suffer the consequences.

If your computer is on a network, you have an additional responsibility to ensure that you do not introduce a computer virus into the network. Computer viruses are programs that can destroy other programs or data.

✦ To reduce the risk of introducing a virus, do not import programs from unknown or disreputable sources.

✦ When you obtain a file or program, follow the proper procedures for checking for viruses before you use it. Check with your system administrator if you have any questions.

✦ Any deliberate attempt to disrupt system performance or data by knowingly spreading a computer virus is considered criminal activity under both state and federal laws.[31]

It is also possible that you may accidentally stumble onto a security problem on your system.

✦ If you identify a possible security problem, immediately notify your system administrator. It will be helpful to this person if you can provide as much information as possible about how you identified the problem.

✦ Do not demonstrate the security problem to anyone other than the system administrator.

✦ Do not go looking for security problems by trying to break into a system or by exceeding your authorized access. This could be construed as an illegal attempt to access a computer system.[32]

---

[31] The Computer Fraud and Abuse Act, a U.S. federal law, has provisions on intentional destructive trespass that cover people who intentionally propagate viruses. Virtually all states have criminal laws that cover the intentional spread of computer viruses.

[32] See the following chapter, "Don't go where you don't belong."

Don't go where you don't belong

Good fences make good neighbors.
Robert Frost

*J*ust as in real life, there are fences and "no trespassing" signs in Cyberspace. They are there for a very good reason—beyond the fences and signs are computer systems that you have no right to be on and information that is, and should remain, private. It is not OK to go where you don't belong, even if you just want to look around or prove you can do it. You are never doing anyone a favor by demonstrating that their computer system is insecure.

Trying to go where you don't belong is also illegal. The following examples are based on U.S. law. Most other countries have laws that make the same actions illegal, though the names of the laws may be different.

✦ The Computer Fraud and Abuse Act, a federal law, makes it illegal to trespass—i.e., make an unauthorized entry—onto an online system or to exceed the bounds of your authorized access to a system. This law also makes it illegal to exchange information about how to gain unauthorized access to a system.

✦ The Electronic Communication Privacy Act, also a federal law, makes it illegal to trespass onto an online system and look at private messages, tamper with those messages, or block others from getting access to their messages. Intentionally disabling a computer system is considered an act that will prevent people from gaining access to their messages.

✦ In addition to federal laws, most states have laws that address the issue of unauthorized access to a computer system. Laws against unauthorized access make it illegal to gain unauthorized entry into a system or to exceed your authorized access on a system. These laws do not require that you harm the system in any way—just being where you don't belong is the basis for finding criminality. State criminal trespass laws make it illegal to make an unauthorized access to a computer system in connection with committing another crime, such as damaging the system or taking computer material.

Some people think that finding ways to break into computer systems is a fun challenge, a way to test their computer skills. The entertainment media has fostered an image of brilliant but mischievous school kids saving the world by breaking into major computer systems. There are ample opportunities to challenge your skills or help save the world that do not involve breaking the law by trying to go where you don't belong.

———

Joe Cracker is a member of a loosely-knit group of folks who are against the growing commercial use of the Net. In an attempt to discourage this trend, Joe has been breaking into commercial computer systems connected through the Net. He does not do any additional damage to the systems other than letting the company know that he was there. He says that his purpose is to prove to companies that the Net is not a safe place for them to be.

What do you think of Joe's actions and logic? What view does the law take of his actions?

Don't pollute

Typical of the subsidiary problems within the whole human survival problem, . . . is the problem of pollution in general—pollution of not only our air and water but also of the information stored in our brains. We will soon have to rename our planet "Poluto."

R. Buckminster Fuller

*A*lways consider the social consequences of what you contribute to the Net. Are you bringing something positive to the Net? Or are you contributing to Cyberspace "pollution"? Our real world is already polluted enough with garbage, toxins, and hatred. Don't be responsible for bringing this darkness into Cyberspace!

Just what is Cyberspace pollution?

+ Material that describes or depicts the sexual abuse and degradation of people or the sexual exploitation of children.

+ Material that promotes hatred towards people because of their race, religion, national origin, sexual preference, gender, and so forth.

+ Profane, rude, obnoxious, harrassing, or offensive speech.

+ Inflammatory speech or personal attacks.

+ Electronic hoaxes, unfounded rumors, or dangerous information, such as instructions on how to build a bomb.

+ Cyberscams, including pyramid schemes, stock scams, and marketing scams.

It is also important to recognize that if an act is illegal in the real world, it is illegal on the Net as well. It has taken a while for the legal authorities to catch on, but they are learning fast, and we can expect increasingly vigorous enforcement of existing laws in Cyberspace.

Watch where you are looking

Unless we change our direction, we are likely to end up where we are going.

Chinese proverb

People who are constantly exposed to negativity cannot help but take on that negativity. It becomes part of them. It colors how they see the world and interact with others. Sometimes people seek out negativity because this is how they feel about themselves and the world around them. While the Net can be an eye to the world, it can also be an eye into ourselves.

What you pay attention to is who you are.

If you are what you eat, then isn't it also true that you are what you consume?

When someone tells you to stop, stop

He who does wrong does wrong against himself. He who acts unjustly acts unjustly to himself because he makes himself bad.

Marcus Aurelius

Harassment is defined as persistently acting in a manner that annoys or distresses another person. Many acceptable use policies, as well as student codes of conduct and employment policies, prohibit harassment. Harassment can also escalate to the level of a criminal offense and can be the basis for a civil suit.

✦ Under most acceptable use policies, messages need not be highly offensive to be considered harassment. If the person who is receiving the messages says it is harassment, it is.[33]

✦ Harassment is generally considered a *repetitive* act. If you send a person one highly offensive message, you may have violated another acceptable use provision, such as using offensive language or making a personal attack.[34] If you send a person more than one message, and the messages are offensive *or* if the person has requested that you stop sending messages, it would be considered harassment.

This very simple rule will help you avoid being accused of online harassment:

Don't send offensive messages. If you are ever told by someone to stop sending him or her messages, stop. Any further messages will constitute harassment.

---

[33] The standards are higher for a criminal or civil action.

[34] Most school and university acceptable use policies prohibit the use of offensive language and personal attacks, and many company and government acceptable use policies also contain such prohibitions.

If it's not true, don't say it

But he that filches from me my good name
Robs me of that which not enriches him
And makes me poor indeed.

William Shakespeare, *Othello*

You do not have the right to say anything you wish about anyone. If you make a false public statement about a person or company that injures the reputation of that person or company, you may have engaged in defamation. There have been recent court cases alleging defamation based on statements posted to discussion groups on the Net, and more cases can be expected as the Net becomes more mainstream. The more people on the Net, the greater the potential for a false statement to cause real damage.

Here are some basic principles of defamation:

✦ The statement must be *false.* Truth is an absolute defense to a defamation claim.

✦ The statement must be *public.* A discussion group would qualify as public communication.

✦ The statement must injure the reputation of the person or company and cause damage.

✦ If you say something about a public figure—a famous person, public official, etc.—you can only be held liable for defamation if you intentionally make a statement that you know is false or if you make the statement with "reckless disregard" for the truth. But watch out for the gray areas regarding who is a public figure and what constitutes "reckless disregard."

✦ It is not defamation if the statement is a "mere opinion," such as an editorial or a statement of personal opinion. Name calling is generally protected as the expression of a personal opinion. But just adding "I think" in front of a defamatory statement will likely not protect you.

To avoid defaming another, consider a slight twist on the old line from your grandmother:

*If you can't think of something truthful to say,
don't say anything at all.*

Unfortunately, the downside of defamation suits is the chilling effect they can have on attempts to bring to light the truly reprehensible activities of companies or individuals—such as exposing their workers to toxic substances or setting up sweatshops that exploit the poor in developing nations. Companies and individuals have been known to bring defamation suits to try to silence those who would question their unacceptable practices. It can work because, truth notwithstanding, the "bad guys" have the financial resources to use the courts to their advantage.

The best advice for those who are committed to trying to make this world a better place by uncovering these unacceptable practices is not to go it alone. Work through an organization that has been established to challenge such practices. Above all, make sure you have done your homework and have the facts on your side.

In a discussion group related to developments in the high-tech industry, a stockbroker posted a message reporting that he had been told of performance problems with XYZtec's new product. The information was incorrect. In response to the message, XYZtec's stock fell dramatically, placing the company in a very perilous financial position.

If you were a juror sitting on the defamation case brought by XYZtec against the stockbroker, how would you evaluate this situation?

Don't take candy from strangers

*t*his section is about being safe on the Net. It is written especially for young people. If you think you are old enough not to be concerned about your safety on the Net, here's a simple test to find out: Have you recently done something that you really didn't want to do because someone else convinced you to do it? If the answer is "yes," you probably should continue reading.

Remember the rule from your childhood, Don't take candy from strangers? It is still a good rule on the Net.

The number of people on the Net who would harm someone is very small, but these people do exist and they could contact you. What's their game? Well, they may be voyeurs, people who find some delight in online discussions of sex or other private matters. Your biggest threat from these people is likely to be shame, embarrassment, and loss of trust in people. While this is not insignificant, it is also not life- or health-threatening.

Other people may present more danger. They are "cyberstalkers" who may try to entice you to meet with them in person, for less-than-desirable reasons and with the potential of a less-than-desirable outcome. It is very important to remember that you cannot see the people you are communicating with on the Internet; therefore, you cannot tell their ages or even their genders. They can tell you anything and you cannot be sure that what they are telling you is true. You may think that you are communicating with someone who is your same age and gender when, in fact, the person is significantly older and the opposite gender.

Cyberstalkers are very likely to use the online equivalent of "candy." They will make a special point of saying very "sweet" things to you, things that make you feel really good. They will usually take your side if you are having any problems with your parents or teachers. What they are doing is trying to earn your confidence and trust by making you feel comfortable communicating with them. This behavior is sometimes called *grooming*. You are being groomed, or flattered, so that you will become willing to do something that you would not otherwise be likely to do.

It is truly a sad world when you have to be suspicious of someone who says nice things to you. It is important to learn to be discerning. There are situations where you deserve praise for what you have accomplished. But if you get the uncomfortable feeling in your gut that something is not quite right, you are probably correct. Trust the feeling!

The following rules are critically important to protect your personal safety:[35]

+ Never give out personal information, such as your address, telephone number, or work address, or your parents' work address or telephone number. This rule is as important for young people who have just moved away from home as it is for young people still at home.

+ If you are a minor, never agree to meet with someone you have met online without checking with a parent. If you are a young person away from home, talk with your parents or a trusted, level-headed friend.

+ If you are a minor and your parent agrees to a meeting, be sure that it is held in a public place and that your parent accompanies you to the meeting. If you are away from home, you should still agree only to meet in a public place and be sure to bring along that trusted, level-headed friend.

+ If anyone ever says to you, "Don't tell anyone" or "Keep this a secret" and you feel at all uncomfortable, it is best to ignore their request. *Do* tell and *don't* keep it a secret.

+ Promptly tell a parent, teacher, or some other trusted person if you receive a message that makes you feel uncomfortable or that you think is inappropriate. Ask for advice on how to handle the situation. You or they may need to send a message to the person telling them to stop contacting you.[36] You may also need to contact your system administrator or the administrator of the system where the messages orginated.

---

[35] Many of these guidelines can be found in an excellent booklet, "Child Safety on the Information Highway," published by The National Center for Missing and Exploited Children (800-843-5678).

[36] See the chapter "Speak up for your rights," on page 61.

✦ Take some positive action if you think you have been approached by an online voyeur or stalker. Save all communications you have received, so that you can provide them to the appropriate authorities. Recognize that if you have been approached, other young people may also be contacted. Your "smarts" and prompt action may help others who are more at risk than you.

The following message was posted on a discussion group: "I am a 24-year-old man. I really like to help young people, young men or young women, with their problems. If you would like to talk with someone who really cares, please write to me. I will be your friend."

What would your discerning response to this kind of message be?

Read between the lines

You have to walk carefully in the beginning of love; the running across fields into your lover's arms can only come later when you're sure they won't laugh if you trip.

Jonathan Carroll

*t*he standard "boy meets girl" (or variation thereof) scenario has taken some interesting turns in Cyberspace. Online relationships are all the rage. Whether the Net is actually the place to find your "soulmate" remains to be seen.

Most of us have grown up hearing very romantic stories of long-distance true love: "He was overseas in the Army. I wrote a letter addressed to 'a soldier.' He responded and we corresponded for 6 months. One week after he came home on leave we were married. We just celebrated our twenty-fifth wedding anniversary." This makes for a nice human interest story and is a good lead-in for advice columnists who want to encourage people to send letters to overseas troops. But these stories have also created an unrealistic fantasy that such scenarios come true frequently. Common sense suggests that the lottery offers better odds.

There are several things to be concerned about with online romances. The first is the danger of being exploited. Cyber pickup artists have developed lines that can equal the best heard in a singles bar. In fact, it is much easier to feign caring, understanding, and commitment via e-mail or chat rooms than it is in real life. Since you don't have the benefit of assessing a person's body language, voice, or other signals that would normally provide some danger signals, you could be easily fooled. But unless you actually meet in person with a cyber pickup artist, the worst that could happen is an emotional roller coaster ride—at least you don't have to worry about sexually-transmitted diseases. If you are going to play the game, you should try to become adept at reading between the lines.

Since it is difficult to tell a cyber pickup artist from others, be sure that you take precautions for your personal safety if you do choose to get together. Pick a public place. Take a friend along, if you can. Don't get into a position where your physical safety could be compromised. And please don't get offended if your online sweetie requests some safety measures.

A second concern is the lack of reality. Online sweeties can take on an image of perfection, especially when compared with "real world" beings who may occasionally have pimples, body odor, or a bad hair day. People may convey one image when online and actually be a very different person when you are face-to-face. Be sure to take the time to get to know the "real person" before you start planning your future together.

Another big concern is unrealistic expectations. If you are lonely, in the throes of a bad relationship, have recently broken up with someone, or are longing to find that one person who will fulfill your every dream, you may be cruising for a bruising. It is important to recognize when you are vulnerable and to protect yourself from unrealistic expectations. It is equally important to recognize when you are communicating with someone who is vulnerable. Don't take advantage of the situation and be sure your expectations of this person are realistic.

On a more positive side, we too often judge others and are judged on the basis of physical appearance. Unfortunately, the vast majority of us fail to reach society's ideal of physical perfection. The Net provides a wonderful opportunity to get to know people on other levels, even very intimate levels. Wouldn't it be wonderful if the Net could lead us into an era where what you have inside and what you have to say is more important than what you look like?

A Net relationship is built on communication—the basic foundation for any healthy relationship. There is no rule that a Net relationship needs to be consummated with a physical relationship. Many people will become life-long Net friends. And maybe, if both people recognize the potential pitfalls, proceed with realistic expectations, and take the time to get to know each other, just maybe, the fantasy could come true.

If it seems too good to be true, it probably is

You can fool some of the people all of the time and all of the people some of the time; but you can't fool all of the people all of the time.

Abraham Lincoln

You can fool too many of the people too much of the time.

James Thurber

A fool and his money are soon parted.

Proverb

*i*t didn't take long for those trying to make a fast buck to find their way into Cyberspace. A growing number of organized rip-offs are occurring on the Net. This chapter describes some of the most common ones.

Credit Card Rip-offs
I work for the accounting department of your Internet access provider. We have lost your credit card number. Will you please send it to me?

You should never provide your credit card number to someone through e-mail. Legitimate companies will not ask you for your credit card number in this manner. The only situation in which it is probably safe to provide your credit card number to someone on the Net is at a secure Web site established by a legitimate company.

Direct Market Sales Scams
You have been *specially* selected to receive this *exclusive offer* to purchase a beautiful 24-carat diamond ring for *only $50.00*. Because this is such a special price, our offer will *end by noon tomorrow*. Don't miss out!!! All major credit cards accepted.

You are right to suspect that any proposed deal that really looks too good to be true—especially if it contains some kind of act-now-or-you-will-lose time limitation—is likely to be a scam.

Pyramid Schemes

Just send a dollar and a recipe to the top five people on the list, add your name to the bottom of the list, and send it on to five more people. Within a week you will be rich beyond your wildest dreams!! This is not an illegal pyramid scheme, it's a recipe exchange.

If it talks like a pyramid scheme and walks like a pyramid scheme, it's a pyramid scheme. It is illegal, and the only people to profit are the ones at the top of the pyramid who find enough fools at the bottom willing to participate in getting fleeced.

Fake Investment Schemes

Make a small investment of $1,000 for stock in a new company that is about to introduce its revolutionary *Weight-Loss Water*. Your small investment is *virtually guaranteed* to quadruple in value in the next several months.

While some companies are beginning to make stock offerings through the Internet, this is an area that has great potential for abuse. Proceed only with great caution if you are interested in investing in a company that provides stock offerings through the Net.

Stock Scams

I have received confidential information from an inside source that Company XYZ is about to launch sales of a widget that will quickly bring in revenues in the multimillions. You can buy their stock at bargain basement prices and score big!

Las Vegas can offer you better odds. Hold onto your wallet.

Don't fall for cyberscams.

Credit the source

Adam was the only man who, when he said a good thing, knew that nobody had said it before him.

Mark Twain

*P*lagiarism—taking ideas or writings from another person and offering them as your own—has always been considered unacceptable. Researching information and incorporating the ideas and writings of others into your work is a very acceptable activity. This is how society has built its base of knowledge.

Because the Net makes it very easy to cut and paste the ideas and writings of other people into your own document, it is important to remember that what distinguishes research from plagiarism is giving credit where credit is due. Never try to pass off anyone else's work as your own.[37]

There are some practical problems when it comes to avoiding plagiarism and doing research on the Net. When you are engaged in Web "surfing" it is very easy to become focused on the ideas and forget to note the sources of those ideas. Backtracking to the source can be very difficult. It is important to anticipate this difficulty before you get started on a project so you can develop a planned, efficient approach to keeping track of your sources. Retaining a separate bookmark file for all of your sources for a specific project is a good way to start.

When you use the work of others it is also important to stay within the bounds of the "fair use exemption" of copyright law.[38]

On the other end of things, those who make their material available on the Net can help by providing citation information directly on the document so that when the document is downloaded or printed, the citation information travels with the document.

---

[37] The two principal guides for citation of material from the Internet are the MLA (Modern Language Association) Style of Citation and the APA (American Psychological Association) Style of Citation. These citation style guides are located on many Web sites.

[38] See the following chapter, "Don't take without permission."

If you are using the Net for research activities, what strategy will you use for keeping track of your sources?

Don't take without permission

Copyright laws are based on an underlying social value that is at the heart of our society:

People have the right to compensation for their creative work.

Why is this considered a beneficial social value? Because compensating people encourages more creative works and our society benefits from these works.

So what is the alternative to copyright laws? Let's imagine a world where a person's creative work automatically becomes the property of society to do with as it wishes. With no chance to sell or market their works, how would creative people pay for their food and rent? Government support? Rich patrons? What kinds of works do you think would be created by people whose only support comes from the government and the wealthy?

One may argue that people really ought to make their works freely available. That's fine, but it is, and should be, the creator's choice to make that decision, and no one else's.

Let's go through some copyright basics.[39] A creative work (text, music, picture, etc.) is automatically protected by copyright from the moment it is created. No copyright notice or registration is required.[40] Therefore, merely publishing a work without a copyright notice is not a relinquishment of copyright. Public domain is the status of a work that is not protected by copyright either because the creator has clearly and specifically relinquished all copyright rights or because the copyright has expired.

The owner of a copyright has exclusive rights to copy, modify, distribute, display, transmit, and perform the work. The owner of a copyright can grant other people permission, called a "license," to exercise any of these rights. The license can be expansive or limited.[41] For example, license to copy and distribute does not mean license to modify or to sell. Transferring a work, in the form of digital data, from one computer system to another is copying and distributing that work and can only be done when there is a license to do so or under specific limiting circumstances.

The "fair use exemption" provides a limited basis by which you can use a copyrighted work without getting permission from the creator. The essence of the fair use exemption is that you are not using the work in a manner that is, or has the potential of, diverting income from the creator.

Generally, it is considered a fair use only if:

✦ You take very little of the copyrighted work;

✦ The portions that you take from the other work constitute a very small part of your work;

✦ Your use of the copyrighted work is for an educational or other socially beneficial purpose; and

✦ Your use of the work does not affect the copyright holder's potential income from his or her work.

Some of the traditional rationales provided for the fair use exemption have been the immediacy of the need for the use of the material for beneficial purposes, the difficulty in contacting the owner of the copyright for permission, and the limited extent of the copying. The ease and speed with which one can

---

[39] If you are creating works and wish to know more about your rights, the U.S. Copyright Office has a series of excellent informational booklets. They are available in hard copy or on the Web at http://lcweb.loc.gov/copyright/.

[40] This is covered under the Berne Convention, an international copyright treaty that the U.S. joined in 1988. However, it is highly advisable for the creator of a work to include a copyright notice.

[41] Shareware and freeware are marketing methods for software that are actually limited licenses. With shareware, the copyright owner has granted permission to copy the program and use it for a trial period. If you want to continue to use it, you must pay a fee. You also have the right to distribute a copy of the program to someone else, provided you do so in its original form and don't charge a fee. With freeware the copyright owner is not requesting a fee for its use. But the program is still protected by copyright. You may not sell or modify it.

communicate directly with the owner of a work on the Net and the expansive potential for publication of material placed on the Net will likely lead to greater restrictions on the ability of people to rely on the fair use exemption.

Ideas are not protected by copyright. Thus, you can write about something that someone else has already written about, as long as you don't use their words or use only a small portion of their words as a direct quote. You should also credit the source of these ideas.[42] You are generally free to write a software program that does what another program does, as long as you don't use the other program's code or its "look and feel."[43]

There are some areas where the extent of copyright protection for material on the Net is unclear.

Much of the material on the Net, including messages and material on Web sites, is protected by copyright. Most people do not specifically grant permission to copy and distribute their material. But the common practice and understanding of people on the Net is that a message posted to a public group can be freely distributed. Technically, to even retrieve a document through the Web requires copying and distributing. Unfortunately, most copyright owners are silent about their intentions with their works.

As might be expected, the Web is too new to find any court cases on these issues. It has been suggested that when the courts review the above issue they may determine that by posting the material in a public discussion group or placing it on a Web site, the creator has granted a limited permission or implied license to copy and distribute for nonprofit purposes, with all other copyright rights retained by the creator.[44] This would not mean that the work has been placed in the public domain, or that you can use for your financial gain something that someone else has published.

But the issue will likely become even more complicated. It is very common to provide links to other pages on the Web. And there may be an implied license to copy and distribute material found on the Web. But can you copy someone else's material, such as a graphic, and put it on your own site? Probably not, but it is possible to establish a link in such a way that someone else's material becomes an integral part of your page. Where have you crossed the line to infringement?

The extent of copyright protection on Web designs is also unclear. A common practice on the Net is to borrow a Web design and use it as a template for your own Web site. But many companies are now spending a significant amount of money developing innovative Web designs, and they are clearly claiming copyright protection for their Web sites. Does the copyright protection extend to the underlying Web design or only the information that is on the site? The answer is unclear. But if you borrow someone's innovative Web

---

[42] See the section "Credit the source," on page 53.

[43] The law on copyright and computer software is complicated. It is best to contact an attorney.

[44] Lance Rose, *Netlaw: Your Rights in the Online World.* Berkeley: McGraw-Hill (1995).

design without getting permission, you might be the one who gets taken to court to help sort out the issues.

Software is now available that will allow you to download complete Web sites and store the material on your server. This capability is useful for schools because it allows a large number of students to quickly access the material without creating a bottleneck on the school's connection. Is this or is this not a violation of copyright?

If you want to place material on your Web site that has been developed by someone else, you are likely to run into difficulties. If you are a student or teacher, there is a slim possibility that your use may fall under the fair use exemption if the materials are only published for the benefit of the class. But the odds are that making materials publicly available would not be considered fair use because this would be considered publishing. If you intend to use commercial clip art on your Web site, make sure that the license will support this use.

Efforts are under way to rewrite copyright laws to take into account technological advances. This will not be an easy or rapid process. It took ten years to rewrite the current U.S. copyright law, which was enacted in 1976.[45] Copyright laws are also clearly an international matter. Any new approach to copyright will require a larger global consensus.[46]

The redefinition of copyright protection in the age of global telecommunication technologies will result in a significant redefinition of property rights for our global information society. In the meantime, we must rely on existing copyright laws and the underlying social value of compensating someone for their creative work. The best advice is to assume that a work is fully protected by copyright and to treat it accordingly. When in doubt—which will be often—about what you can or cannot do with a particular work:

Ask permission from the creator of the work.

Fortunately, on the Net, it is quite easy to send the creator an e-mail message specifying how you propose to use his or her work and requesting permission to do so.

It would also be very helpful for those who are creating works and posting them on the Net to be clear about the rights they are claiming and what uses

---

[45] And it almost didn't get enacted, because it was pointed out at the last minute that the law made no reference to computer software programs. This reference was added to the 1976 law basically as a "placeholder." In 1978, the copyright act was amended to specifically address computer software.

[46] In September 1995, the U.S. Working Group on Intellectual Property Rights of the Clinton administration's National Information Infrastructure issued a *White Paper on Intellectual Property and the NII*. Other countries are also issuing similar papers. The World Intellectual Property Organization is sponsoring a series of meetings to discuss issues related to digital technology. Most countries appear to recognize the need for a harmonization of the world's copyright laws—but they want to harmonize on their country's terms.

of their materials they consider acceptable. This way creators will not be bothered by requests for permission to use their works. A simple statement, placed on the work, should do the trick. For example:

> © 199_, *creator's name.* Permission granted to copy and distribute in electronic or hard copy form for nonprofit purposes only. All other rights retained by the author. If you have any questions, please contact the creator at: *e-mail address.*

> © 199_, *creator's name.* The copyright protection extends only to the material—text and graphics—that is contained on this site. Permission is granted to incorporate aspects of the Web design into your sites.

Perhaps while the big policy wonks fight this out, a culture of respect for copyrighted works can begin to flourish on the Net.

———————

In your opinion, what are the basic principles that ought to be incorporated into copyright law to make it work effectively on the Net?

speak up for your rights

A good indignation brings out one's powers.

Ralph Waldo Emerson

It is better to be a lion for a day than a sheep all your life.

Elizabeth Heary

Never go to bed mad.
Stay up and fight.

Phyllis Diller

Some people think that the Net gives them the freedom to do anything they want—treat people rudely, violate their privacy, harass them, and so on. They think they should have the freedom to ignore other people's rights.

You have the right to use the Net without being subjected to such treatment. You may, on occasion, have to speak up for your rights. When you do speak up, your complaints may be met with anguished cries of "Censorship!" or "You're trying to take away my freedom!" But if you know you are in the right, stand your ground. The Net will be a better place for it.

✦ *You have a right not to receive harassing or offensive e-mail.*
If you receive any message that makes you uncomfortable or that you feel is unacceptable, send the source of the message a terse reply: "Stop sending me messages." If you receive a message that a reasonable person would consider offensive or if you continue to receive messages after telling someone to stop, contact your system administrator for assistance in dealing with the situation. Be sure to save all the messages you have received and sent.

Most educational institutions and employers have policies against harassment and offensive messages. Many commercial providers will also terminate the account of a user who behaves in such a manner.

✦ *You have a right to privacy.*
You have a right not to have personal information about you disclosed to others in e-mail form. Your private messages to a person should not be forwarded without your express consent.

61

If your right to privacy has been violated inadvertently, you may wish to deal with the situation by pointing out the violation to the other person and requesting that he or she not repeat the action. If the violation was particularly egregious, you may be able to seek remedies through the system you are on. Many education systems have policies against violations of privacy.

You also have rights to privacy of your personal files, although these rights may be limited depending on the type of system you are using. On commercial systems you should have a right to privacy unless your provider has specifically informed you otherwise. If your account is provided by your school or employer, they probably have the right to investigate the contents of your personal files.[47] But even on school or employer systems, you should have a right to some form of due process if the contents of your personal files are to be accessed by others.[48]

✦ *You have proprietary rights to your own creative works.*
You determine the extent to which you give people the right to copy and distribute your creative works. Just because you place your material on the Net doesn't mean that you have given up your copyright rights. It is most prudent to include a copyright notice that clearly states the rights you retain and what actions are permissible with your creative works.

✦ *You have a right not to have untrue things said about you on the Net.*
If an untruth is published about you on the Net that you feel has the potential to cause significant harm to your reputation, your career, and so on, it is best to contact an attorney for advice on how to handle the matter. Sometimes, the proper response is simply to demand a retraction. But sometimes harm has been done and you may have a case for damages.

✦ *If you are a student working in a computer lab established by your educational institution, you have a right not to be subjected to images of pornography.*
Your right to use a computer that has been provided for your education in a nonhostile, nonharassing environment is clearly superior to whatever rights other students may feel they have to view pornography, an activity that has no educational value. You are not violating anyone's rights to free speech by saying, "This technology has been provided to serve an educational purpose, and so, in this environment, pornography is not acceptable."

Your school's code of student conduct should provide sufficient basis for a complaint based on harassment or offensive conduct. If your institution does not have a specific policy that prohibits such activities in a computer lab, then it should. Unfortunately, some educational institutions are in need of some "consciousness-raising" on this issue. It may be safer to tackle this issue through a women's center, university ombudsperson, or

---

[47] See the section "Tread carefully," on page 21.

[48] If you are an employee or an elected official and your account is on a government system, your right to privacy is overridden by citizen rights of access to public records.

with the assistance of a sympathetic faculty member. If an institution fails to prevent such harassment, a suit for sex discrimination under Title IX of the Education Amendments of 1972 may also be in order.

✦ *You have the right not to receive unwanted junk e-mail and to protect your children from commercial exploitation.*
Irresponsible companies and individuals have discovered the potential of the Net for the distribution of marketing materials. Some companies are establishing sites that are attractive to children in order to solicit from children information about their interests and their family's interests to be used for the purpose of targeted marketing. Other companies are sending unsolicited junk e-mail. We should have the right to be free from such speech.

While we can support legislation that will restrict abuse of the Net for commercial purposes, we can also take personal action by taking the time to respond to those who abuse the Net resources in such a manner. One Netizen suggested the following approach if you receive unwanted junk e-mail: Write your objection to the receipt of such junk e-mail and send 10 copies of this objection to the source of the offending junk e-mail. Also send 10 copies of your objection to the system administrator. Address the message to the system administrator as follows: postmaster@ ___ (the domain name portion of the junk e-mail source).[49]

Providers of Net blocking software and those creating rating systems for questionable material on the Net could do parents a real favor by publishing with the list of "indecent" sites a list of the "commercial exploitation" sites that have been established to entice our children for the purposes of selling them products.

A female student is doing work in a university computer lab. A male student sits at the computer next to hers and begins to download pornography. The female student complains and an argument ensues. The dispute is referred to the director of computer services, who responds, "What we have here is a conflict of rights. Her right to do her work in a nonharassing environment and his right to view whatever material he wants."

What is your assessment of this view of a "conflict of rights"?[50]

---

[49] Possible language for a letter of objection: I suggest you find some other way to "advertise" your business. Many of us are becoming very upset that we are being bombarded daily with "junk mail" such as yours. Without invitation, you have taken my valuable time (and have cost me money because I have to pay for the receipt of messages, whether I want them or not). I encourage all my friends, colleagues, contacts, etc., *not* to do business with people who advertise as obnoxiously as you do! I will also fully support legislation that will begin to restrict such activities. Please reconsider and find a more respectful way to use the Internet for your business purposes.

[50] This is an actually reported incident. Out of courtesy to the institution, I am declining to identify the source.

get a life

What's the matter with these people?
Don't they have a life?

Netism

One honest answer to the question "Don't these people have lives?" is that most people don't have a terribly glamorous life. They work, they subsist, they are lonely or afraid or shy or unattractive or feel they are unattractive. Or they are simply different.

Harold Reingold

*a*re you lost in Cyberspace?

✦ You went away for three days and returned to find 1,892 messages in your mailbox.

✦ You just came out of the computer room and your dog is barking at you as if you were a stranger.

✦ You just missed your daughter's soccer game, your son's piano recital, or your best friend's wedding because you were traveling the information superhighway.

✦ Your family thinks you moved out a year ago.

All joking aside, it is possible to overdo things. And it's important to know where to draw the limits. As fun as the Net can be, take a real close look at yourself if playing on the Net ranks as a higher priority than your family and friends or your schoolwork or work. Humankind does not live by bits and bytes alone.

✦ Have a purpose for using the Net. While recreation is a worthwhile purpose, make sure you recreate wisely. Remember that recreation literally means to "re-create." You should come away from recreational activities invigorated and energized, not drained.

✦ Don't participate in more discussion groups than you can handle. If you find yourself frequently deleting unread messages, this is a strong clue that you may have signed up for too much. Participate in groups that make a valuable contribution to your life and are either moderated or use self-restraint to keep out the "noise."

✦ If you feel you are spending too much time on the Net, consider setting daily time limits. At first, you might just keep track of the amount of time you spend. The results may surprise you.

✦ Avoid using the Net to escape from your real-world problems. If you find that you often want to break away from activities with real people to go and lose yourself in Cyberspace, you might want to consider what this says about your relationship with the people around you.

✦ If your use of the Net is interfering with your family life, schoolwork, or work, it has reached the stage where it is causing harm. It's time to reorganize your priorities.

Expand your mind

When I learn something new—and it happens every day—I feel a little more at home in the universe, a little more comfortable in the nest.

Bill Moyers

Nothing is more dangerous than an idea when it is the only one you have.

Emile Chartier

*A*re you in a Cyberspace rut? Have you gotten into a familiar online routine—just this group of online friends, just these discussion groups, just these Web sites? Have you found a comfortable little corner of Cyberspace to hang out in?

Wake up! The whole world is at your fingertips! Get out and explore. Expand your horizons beyond your own little virtual corner. Take the time to meet new people, to understand their culture and their perspectives on the events of the day. Be curious. Consider some new possibilities.

Let's get practical here. How does one move beyond a comfortable little corner in Cyberspace? Here's one strategy:

- ✦ Sit down and make a list of all the things that you're interested in. Come on now, aren't there a few more things you can add to the list?

- ✦ Each week, take some time to explore one of your interests. Pick an item from your list and explore the Web for an hour to find what is out there that relates to this interest. Or you might want to see if there are any discussion groups on this subject. Don't make a long-term commitment to yet another group—but sign up and lurk for a week just to check out the new scene.

- ✦ As you explore, you may find new things of interest to add to your list.

Scientists tell us that every time we learn something new, we create new dendrites, those little connections within our brain that enable us to think and process information. It's simple—the more connections, the more brain power.

Read with your eyes open

The problem with the information age, especially for students and knowledge workers who spend their time immersed in the info flow, is that there is too much information and very few effective filters for sifting the key data that are useful and interesting to us as individuals.

Harold Reingold

With the glut of information on the Net, determining what information is correct and what is not clearly poses a major problem for users. Unfortunately, in the information age, we will still be faced with a task from the agricultural age: separating the wheat from the chaff!

Here are some guidelines for assessing the accuracy of the information you may find on the Net:

✦ Start with the recognition that there are no "Cyberspace Truth Monitors"— no one making sure that the things people tell you or the information you find is accurate and true. You will need to make your own judgements.

✦ Consider the source of the information. Is your information service provided by a university department, a person with acknowledged expertise in the field, a government agency, or a well-respected social service organization? If you have received a response to a question you posted, who is the response from and what is this person's apparent background or expertise in the subject area?

✦ Determine whether the information is consistent with information obtained through other sources. Is the same information present at several locations? Have you received several consistent responses to your question?

✦ Consider how you got to the information. Did you get to it by following a pointer from a recognized high-quality information resource, such as a library homepage, a suggested reading list for a university class, or a resource list maintained by a credible organization or an individual known for his or her expertise in the field?

✦ Seek out others who have an interest or expertise in this area, such as a relevant discussion group, and ask for their opinions. What do you think of this document? Of this source? Of this response to my question?

✦ Evaluate the substance of the information itself. Is the material internally coherent? Is it logical? Is it consistent with what you already know to be true? Does it "feel" right?

Share your expertise

Each act makes us manifest. It is what we do, rather than what we feel, or say we do that reflects who and what we truly are. Each of our acts makes a statement as to our purpose. Whatever immortality there is, is assured by a continual participation in the productive process. Because of us, things have become more. Something has been left of significance because we existed.

Leo Buscaglia

*O*ne reason the Net is such an incredibly wonderful place is the millions of people who are making contributions and sharing their expertise. The pure wonder of this technology is that it provides people with the opportunity to give as well as to receive.

Jump on board and share your expertise. There are many ways that you can contribute:

✦ Offer answers and help to people who ask questions.

✦ Show a clueless newbie the way.

✦ If you receive several e-mail answers to a question you have posted to a discussion group, take the time to compose an easily readable summary of the responses and post it back to the group.

✦ If you are a longtimer in a group or have some special expertise, consider writing a FAQ for the group.

✦ Be a good facilitator. Sometimes discussions bog down, slow down, or get off track. You can do your part to promote the flow of quality information by raising an appropriate topic for discussion or by asking questions that lead to a deeper, more informative discussion.

✦ Be a mediator. If you sense that a discussion is getting too heated—and especially if there appear to be misunderstandings among some participants—help to cool the issue off a bit. Calmly ask some questions. Focus on the subject. Honor the passion people feel with respect to the issue, but discourage the personal attacks and inflammatory language.

✦ If you have special expertise and have written papers or conducted research, consider establishing a Web site to share your knowledge with others.

✦ If you are affiliated with a nonprofit organization that has information that could be of interest to others, volunteer your time to establish a Web site for the organization.

✦ Just because you're a young person doesn't mean you don't have anything to share. You may know much more about a particular subject than most people and you can share your knowledge through your own Web site. Don't be afraid to participate in conversations where people appear to be older than you. Your thoughts and perceptions are important, too.

Lend a helping hand

> I do not know what your destiny will be, but one thing I do know: the only ones among you who will be really happy are those who have sought and found how to serve.
>
> Albert Schweitzer

> It is one of the most beautiful compensations of life that no man can sincerely try to help another without helping himself.
>
> Ralph Waldo Emerson

*t*hink of the many, many people in your community who have not yet connected to this brave new world. They are not clueless newbies—they are still just clueless! If you have achieved a level of comfort on the Net, look around and see where you can lend a helping hand. Many schools, libraries, community networks, and community centers are now establishing connections to the Internet. They would probably welcome someone to help teach people how to use the Net. Here are some suggestions for helping people learn to use the Net:

✦ Slow down. People who are just starting on the Net need to take their time; if you move too fast, you will lose them. If you are a young person, remember that you have grown up with computers and feel comfortable with them. Many older people are still not comfortable with computers.

✦ Make sure that the people you are helping have their fingers on the keyboard. Don't show them—tell them what to do and then allow them to do it for themselves.

✦ Be sensitive to the needs of the person you are helping. Expect to be asked the question "Why" and do your best to answer it in nontechnical terms with something other than "Because that is how it works." Many people need to understand *why* something works the way it does to be able to remember *how* to do it. On the other hand, some people may not want to know *why* something works the way it does. They just want to know *how.*

✦ Take newbies to where their interests are. Start by signing them up on a mailing list related to their interest. Mailing lists are substantially less intimidating than newsgroups and have a more personal feel because the mail is "delivered." People-to-people contact through a mailing list is also more personal than just surfing Web pages.

✦ Provide continual assurances that there is no way that the newbie can break anything on the Net or on the computer. Many adults fear that if they push the wrong button they will destroy everything.[51]

✦ Watch your students for signs of burnout—glazed eyes are a good clue—and send them out for recess when they appear to need a break.

---

[51] Hey, give us a break! When we were growing up, we had to practice ducking under our desks to avoid annihilation in the event of an atomic attack. We have a great respect for buttons that might destroy.

Feel the funk, but do it anyway

Future shock is the dizzying orientation brought about by the premature arrival of the future.

Alvin Toffler

Toto, I don't think we are in Kansas anymore.

Dorothy, *Wizard of Oz*

When we enter Cyberspace, we are bombarded with a dizzying array of information input. We feel that we have left behind the world that was tangible and real. We experience an erosion of our sense of place, time, and body. It is disorienting and somewhat strange. Many of us who are on the Net feel almost as if we are moving at an entirely different time rate—Cyberspeed. This may create tension when dealing with people who are still functioning in earth time. This time warp makes it difficult for us to know "when" we are.

The explosion of information can be overwhelming. Sure, you can find the answers to many questions on the Net, but only if you know how to locate the exact piece of information you need and are able to distinguish good information from bad. The increased availability of information does not appear to be making life more understandable; rather, it is increasing the level of ambiguity that we must deal with. The answers are not in black and white, they are in myriad shades of gray. The complexities of life seem only to be getting more complex.

In addition, electronic communication is bringing us much closer to the tragedy that is present in our world. Our ancestors might not hear of tragic events until months or years after they had unfolded. In more recent times, our news media has brought us up-to-the-minute pictures and interviews from the scene. But the Net can bring us even closer, through the exchange of personal messages with real people who are living the tragedy. Too often, though, we feel that all we can do is share their pain, because we are powerless to have any effect on the outcome of the events.

Will all this disconcerting change resolve itself soon? Not likely. We are just on the threshold of the transition to the information age. The pace of change can only be expected to quicken. Society's major institutions—government, education, and business—are still basically functioning with industrial age organizational structures and processes. Things are starting to shift, but this is only "incremental change." We are still just rearranging the deck chairs on the industrial age Titanic. What we are moving toward in the not-too-distant future is "discontinuous change," a radical shift in the organizational structure and activities of society's institutions.

How will we survive all of this? The two traits that it will be most helpful to cultivate are:

◆ *Patience*
   Life may be changing rapidly, but some situations and some people will simply not change as rapidly as we might wish. Unfortunately, there will be little to nothing that we can do but to have patience; patience with the process, patience with other people, and, most importantly, patience with ourselves.

◆ *Action*
   Other situations may require more active involvement; that is, taking the personal responsibility to make things better. It is amazing what can be accomplished when individuals take the initiative to do something about a bad situation. The Net can be very empowering for those who have the courage to take responsibility for making this world a better place.

How could you use the Net to make this world a better place for others?

We are one world

The eyes and ears of our telecommunications network are becoming the eyes and ears of humanity, allowing us to share new sets of experiences. And as our experiences expand, so does our awareness of ourselves and our environment. We are becoming increasingly aware that we are all fellow passengers on "Spaceship Earth." We are a single species, sharing not only a common home, but also a common destiny.

Peter Russell

*O*ur global society will undergo extraordinary change in our lifetime. We are rapidly moving into an era where physical boundaries will be irrelevant; an era where neither rules nor laws, authority figures nor technological barriers will be wholly successful in controlling behavior. We will have to rely on the most important control of all—the control that comes from within each of us.

Consider what the implications would be for our global society if the dominant ethical standard of the information age was based on the philosophy of "If I can get away with it, I will." Our very existence would be jeopardized. We, as citizens of this planet, will either come together to face the challenges of tribalism, environmental destruction, and human rights for all people, or we will be pulled apart.

The Net can be the tie that binds us together. But because the Net is a place of freedom, we—each of us—will have to make a choice about the kinds of ethics that will guide our personal actions both on the Net and in the real world.

Our use of the Net will reflect who we are.

Glossary

This Glossary contains Net-related terms that have been used in this book as well as other terms that users may encounter upon their travels in Cyberspace.

@ The @ is used to separate the username and the domain name in an Internet address. It is read as "at." The text to the right of the @ is the specific user account name. The text to the left is the domain name of the Internet provider.

* 1) When used in a message, the * indicates that a *special* emphasis should be given to a word because it is *really* important. Considered the equivalent of boldfaced type. 2) When used in a search program the * symbolizes a wildcard.

? When used in a search program the ? symbolizes a wildcard.

/ Directory separator. When used in an URL the / denotes different directories.

~ When used in an URL, the ~ denotes a directory that is associated with a particular username.

_ The underline is used in messages to denote words that should be italicized or underlined. It is generally used to indicate the name of a publication. In an e-mail message this book would be referred to as _The Cyberethics Reader_.

acceptable use policy (AUP) The acceptable use policy is a document prepared by the Internet provider outlining the kinds of activities that are or are not acceptable on this provider's system.

access To connect to or interact with a computer.

account The user ID and personal files restricted to the use of a particular person.

address or IP address (Internet Protocol address) 1) Generally, when people use the term *address* they are referring to an e-mail address, also called a user address. 2) Technically, the address or IP address is the specific number sequence that identifies a computer or other device on the

Internet. The address is made up of four sets of numbers separated by dots, e.g., 123.456.789.12. Because mere mortals have difficulty remembering a long series of numbers, IP addresses have a corresponding text version called a domain name or an alias. *See also* alias, domain name.

alias 1) The text version of a numerical IP address. *See also* address, domain name. 2) A feature of most e-mail programs that allows you to establish a short alias or nickname for individuals or for personal distribution lists. When you use this feature all you need to type in the address section is the alias. The software automatically fills in the full e-mail address of the individual or all of the e-mail addresses of the people on your personal distribution list. 3) A username that does not clearly identify the user. *See also* handle.

alt (Alternative Newsgroups) The Usenet newsgroup category that has no manner of control; the online embodiment of anarchy. *See also* newsgroups.

Anonymous FTP (file transfer protocol) An Internet application that allows you to access a public collection of files on a remote host without having to have a personal account on the remote system. Anonymous FTP was the first-generation capability to provide general access to material through the Internet. Gopher was the second generation. World Wide Web is the third generation. *See also* file transfer protocol.

applet A small application program written in JAVA language that can be downloaded with a Web document to add programmable features to Web pages. *See also* JAVA.

archive A repository of files, e.g., an FTP archive or a collection of messages from a discussion group.

article A single news item or message posted to a newsgroup. *See also* newsgroups.

ASCII (American Standard Code for Information Interchange) A standard that assigns 7-bit codes to 128 different elements, including letters of the alphabet, numbers, and punctuation marks. ASCII is the standard means for transferring text-only files—including e-mail—across the Internet.

asynchronous Not occurring at the same time. On the Internet, except in IRC or talk, group discussions such as mailing lists and newsgroups are asynchronous. The nice thing about this is that you can engage in conversation with other people when you have the time, and do not have to wait for others to be available. *Contrast* real time.

attachment A file that is sent along with an e-mail message. The attached file can be text or binary.

backbone A high performance network that connects other networks.

bandwidth The amount of data or traffic that can be transmitted through a circuit. The greater the bandwidth, the more data the line can handle.

baud The speed of a modem. The higher the number, the faster the speed.

bcc (blind carbon copy) An e-mail feature that allows you to send a copy of a message to an individual without alerting the other recipient(s) that you have done so. Be warned, though, that the bcc feature is not compatible across all systems. On some systems, the bcc recipient may be listed in the header. If it is very important that your blind copy recipient not be identified, it is best to first send the message to the intended recipient and then forward a separate copy of your message to your blind copy recipient. (It's interesting that a term that originally referred to a copy made on a manual typewriter with a messy black piece of paper is still in use today.) *See also* cc.

binary file A nonASCII file containing data that is not text and therefore cannot be printed. Binary files contain graphics, sound, and programs.

body The part of the e-mail that contains the message. *Contrast* header.

bookmark A feature of Web browsers that allows you to store the URL address of a Web site so that you can easily find it again. *See also* browser.

Boolean search A search method that makes use of operators, such as *and, or,* and *not,* to define relationships between the keywords listed in the search string. *See also* keywords, operators.

bot A program that watches an IRC channel and automatically responds when certain messages are posted.

bounce The return of an e-mail message that could not be delivered because of an error in its addressing or delivery. The remote system postmaster software will return the message to you with information about why the message bounced. However, since the postmaster software speaks only computerese, the message may be hard to decipher.

broadcast message A message sent to all of the users on a system.

browser or Web browser A utility that allows you to look through collections of data. The Web is accessed through the use of Web browsers, such as Netscape.

bug An error in the software that causes a problem.

cache An area where information is retained temporarily for rapid access. When you select Web pages, the browser retains the pages in a cache so that you can return to them quickly. When you terminate your Web access, your browser cleans out the cache.

cc (carbon copy) A feature of e-mail programs that allows you to list additional people who are to receive a copy of the message. Note, however, that e-mail programs also allow you to list corecipients. There appears to be little difference between a corecipient and a person who receives a cc'd message. The generally accepted approach is to list those people who really need to see a message and ought to respond as corecipients and to cc people who are secondary in importance and are not expected to respond. *See also* bcc.

CFV (Call For Votes) Part of the process of setting up a new newsgroup. When a new newsgroup is proposed there will be some discussion, and then a call for votes. Participants vote to determine whether there is enough interest to justify setting up the new group. *See also* newsgroups.

channel A conversation group related to a particular subject in the Internet Relay Chat. Similar to a Usenet newsgroup or conference on a commercial online provider; the difference is that the conversation in a channel occurs in real time, while newsgroups and conferences are asynchronous. *See also* IRC.

charter A statement of the name, topic, and guidelines for a newsgroup. *See also* newsgroups.

chat An online interactive talk program that allows people to communicate in real time by typing messages to each other. *See also* talk and IRC.

client A device or program that is able to make use of another device or program, called a server, to accomplish a task. *See also* server, client/server computing.

client/server computing A model for how computers work together on a network. In the client/server model both the client and the server have specialized software that is complementary and permits the two computers to actively work with each other to accomplish a task. *See also* client, server. *Contrast* terminal/host computing.

Clipper Chip A chip (integrated circuit) that contains encryption standards recommended by the U.S. National Security Agency. The advocates for the Clipper Chip state that such a system is necessary to ensure that law enforcement officials will be able to monitor potentially illegal data traffic. Opponents are concerned that abuse of the technology will lead to invasion of personal privacy.

com The domain name that refers to commercial organizations. Probably a U.S. site. *See also* domain.

comp The Usenet newsgroup category that discusses topics related to computers. *See also* newsgroups.

compression A technology that reduces the size of a file, thereby reducing bandwidth demands when transmitting the file and disk space when storing it. *Contrast* extraction.

congestion Too much traffic. When the amount of data being transmitted exceeds the capacity of the transmission facilities.

connect time The amount of time you are online. Some commercial providers may charge you based on your connect time.

country code The two-character domain that identifies the country of the site; for example, "us" is the United States and "ca" is Canada. *See also* domain.

cracker A person who tries to break into a computer system. *Contrast* hacker.

cross-posting Posting the same message to several newsgroups or mailing lists. This can create congestion and is not considered appropriate by some groups. However, cross-posting may be justified when more than one discussion group would be interested in the subject matter of the message.

CWIS (Campus Wide Information Server) A CWIS is an information service that contains information about a particular university or college. The CWIS is usually a Web site.

Cyberspace A world in which people and computers coexist. When you are on the Internet, you are in Cyberspace. The word first appeared in *Necromancer*, a science fiction novel by William Gibson.

decode To transfer a file from an encoded format to its original format. *Contrast* encode.

device A piece of equipment, such as a computer or printer.

dial-up The use of a modem to connect to a provider through phone lines.

digest A single file that contains many messages. Some mailing lists offer users the opportunity to receive a digest of messages that have been posted to the list. This substantially reduces the cost to people who pay by the message on their service. Some folks also prefer to read through all of the messages at one time, rather than following the ongoing flow of the dialog. People who lurk are more apt to use digests.

directory A structure that is used to organize files or documents. The address for a document contains the directory structure with subdirectories separated by a / (slash). A real world analogy for a directory structure would be telling someone to find a document by following these instructions: office 123/file cabinet B/file drawer 3/file folder red/document name. The URL for a Web page contains the directory structure to locate the documents.

discussion group An electronically distributed forum in which people can discuss issues and share information. A general term that covers both mailing lists and Usenet newsgroups. *See also* mailing list, newsgroups.

distribution list A feature of most e-mail programs that allows you to create a personal distribution list. You are able to list all the individual usernames and addresses you want to include and then give the whole list one alias or nickname. When you type the alias into the header, the e-mail program automatically sends the message to every person on the list. Unlike a mailing list, which is a many-to-many service sent by a remote system, a distribution list is a one-to-many process controlled by an individual user. *See also* alias.

domain The highest subdivision of the domain name hierarchy that appears as the last part of a domain name. For the most part, the domain is a two-character code that identifies the country, such as "uk" for the United Kingdom. In the U.S., the domain was traditionally a three-character descriptive code, "edu" for educational, "mil" for military, "org" for miscellaneous organizations, "gov" for government, "com" for commercial, and "net" for network resources. More recently, sites in the U.S. have begun to use the country domain, "us".

domain name The full hierarchical name for a host on the Internet, the domain name is the text equivalent of the IP address. It is what appears to the right of the @ sign in an address. The domain name reads from the specific to the general. It may include the name of the host computer, the site to which the computer is attached, and the Internet domain. *See also* address.

download To move data from a remote computer to your computer. *Contrast* upload.

downstream Usenet newsgroup feeds travel from computer to computer. The computer that receives a Usenet feed from a host computer is considered to be downstream from the host. *Contrast* upstream.

downtime or **down** When a network or computer system is inoperative. If the system is down you will not be able to access it.

e-journal A regularly published electronic journal, typically targeted at academic audiences. Some journals are published both in hard copy and online. Online journals can be distributed less expensively and are more easily searchable than hard copy journals.

e-mail An electronic message delivered from one person to another.

e-mail address An e-mail address consists of the username, the @ sign, and the domain name of the Internet provider. Another name for e-mail address is user address.

e-zine An electronic magazine that may or may not be regularly published. E-zines cover a wide range of topics. An updated list of e-zines is published regularly on atl.zines, and many e-zines are also available on Web sites.

edu The domain name that refers to educational institutions. Probably a U.S. site. *See also* domain.

emoticons Emotional icons. Because it is difficult to convey emotions in straight text, people frequently use emoticons to add emotional coloring to what they are saying. *See also* smileys.

encode To transfer a file from one form to another. *Contrast* decode.

encryption A security technique that makes a file unintelligible to anyone who does not have the authorization and encryption key to access it.

expire Remove an article from a newsgroup after a specified time. *See also* newsgroups.

extracting Uncompressing a compressed file. *Contrast* compression.

FAQ (Frequently Asked Questions) file A FAQ file contains the most commonly asked questions and answers that appear on a discussion group. The purpose of the file is to answer newcomers' questions without wasting the time of long-term participants of the group who have grown weary of explaining the same things over and over.

feed *See* newsfeed.

file A collection of information or data that is treated as a unit by the computer.

file extension A suffix that follows a filename and shows what type of file it is. Some common filename extensions are: txt—a text file, gif—pictures in graphic interchange format, and jpeg—a JPEG-compressed image.

filter A feature of e-mail programs that enables the user to filter mail into specific folders or directories based on the words contained in the message header, subject line, or body of the message.

finger A program that provides personal information about users on an Internet host.

flame A term that has a range of meanings from impassioned statements to rude, obnoxious, and inflammatory ones.

flame bait An intentionally inflammatory message designed to offend other readers and incite a flame war.

flame war A long-running exchange of inflammatory postings.

folder A structure used to group similar items together. Most e-mail programs allow you to create folders to store your mail.

follow-up or **follow-on** A reply to a previous post. A series of follow-ups constitutes a thread. *See also* thread.

forms A Web feature that allows the person accessing a Web page to fill in information on a data entry sheet.

forward A feature of e-mail programs that enables a user who has received a message to send it to another person.

freeware Software that you can use and distribute at no charge. The owner still owns the copyright. *See also* shareware, public domain.

ftp (file transfer protocol) A TCP/IP protocol that permits a file to be transferred from one computer to another. The development of the ftp protocol solved the problem of transferring files between different kinds of computer systems. *See also* Anonymous FTP.

GIF or **gif (Graphic Interchange Format)** 1) (uppercase letters) A compressed graphic file format; a bit-map graphic file. 2) (lowercase letters) The file extension for a picture in graphic interchange format. *See also* file extension.

glitches Brief, intermittent failures of indeterminate cause. Hardware has glitches, software has bugs.

Gopher A menu-driven system that lets you access archives of information on Internet hosts that provide a Gopher service. The Gopher "goes for" the item selected from the menu. Gopher has largely been displaced by the Web, but documents stored on a Gopher server are also accessible through the Web.

gov The domain name that refers to government sites. Probably a U.S. site. *See also* domain.

groupware Software programs that support group activities, such as scheduling, group conferencing, and collaborative work products.

hacker The term *hacker* has taken on various meanings. Some people distinguish a cracker, who attempts to break into computer systems to create harm, from a hacker, who just wants to break into the system to prove it can be done. Both of these actions are illegal. Other people define a cracker as anyone who attempts to break into systems, regardless of whether they intend to do harm, and a hacker as anyone who has an intimate understanding of computers and networks and who could break into computer systems, but does not. *Contrast* cracker.

handle A nickname or username alias. Some users adopt a handle for their username. Others may adopt a handle when playing games on the Net. *See also* alias.

header The portion of an e-mail message that contains the sender, recipient, subject, and the origination date and time. *Contrast* body.

hit A match to the criteria or keywords that you specify in a database or Web search. *See also* keywords.

homepage 1) The primary Web page for an individual or organization. The homepage provides links to other pages that relate to that site. 2) The document your Web browser loads when it starts up. It should contain links that you use frequently.

host 1) A specific computer or computer system that is connected to the Internet, the host computer usually serves more than one user. The computer established by an Internet provider is the host for the users on that system.

A local host is one that a user accesses through dial-up or through a computer that is connected to it. A remote host is accessed through the local host. 2) A more specific use of the term refers to computers that are configured to work with dumb terminals. The host does all of the computing work and the terminal is used for input and output. *See also* terminal, terminal host computing.

host name The unique name that identifies a host computer. The host name is the left-most name of the domain name, appearing directly to the right of the @ sign in a user address.

hot list A list of favorite Web sites that can be accessed quickly by your Web browser. *See also* bookmark.

HTML (Hypertext Markup Language) The language used to create Web pages on the Web. HTML controls both how the page will appear (although this may differ depending on the browser) and the special features of the page, such as links to other pages and forms. *See also* Web page.

hypermedia A document that contains a mix of different media—text, graphics, sound, and animation.

hypertext A document that contains links that make connections to other documents so that a multidimensional work is created as opposed to a linear work. The Web is a hypertext system.

Internet The global network of networks that all speak the same language known as TCP/IP.

IP (Internet Protocol) The protocol or rules that control how data is routed between hosts on the Internet.

IP address (Internet Protocol address) *See* address.

IRC (Internet Relay Chat) IRC enables groups of people from throughout the world to engage in real-time conversations through the Net. While IRC is frequently used for idle conversation, it can be used for more serious activities, such as business conferences and educational projects. One valuable feature of the technology is that the entire online conversation can be saved for future reference. *See also* talk, chat.

JAVA A language that allows small applications, called applets, to be downloaded within a Web document to add programmable features to Web pages. *See also* applet.

jpeg A file extension for JPEG-compressed images. JPEG stands for Joint Photography Experts Group. *See also* file extensions.

keywords Words entered into a search query that describe the information sought. Keywords are separated by operators that define the relationship between the words. They may also contain wildcards. Different search engines use different methods to specify operators and wildcards. *See also* search engine, operators, wildcard.

kill file A newsreader feature that allows the user to specify criteria that will automatically filter out certain messages, generally by subject, author, or words. Messages from people who frequently flame or who waste other people's time often end up in kill files.

knowbots Programs that automatically search through a network for specific information.

LAN (Local Area Network) A group of computers that are located in one area and are connected through cabling. If two or more LANs are connected with each other over a wider geographical area it is called a Wide Area Network (WAN). *Contrast* WAN.

links Words or graphics in a hypertext document, such as a Web page, that cause another document to be accessed when they are selected. *See also* pointer.

list A common abbreviation of mailing list. Originally referred to as a LISTSERV mailing list. *See also* LISTSERV, mailing list.

Listproc An automatic mailing list distribution system. *See also* mailing list.

LISTSERV An automatic mailing list distribution system that runs on an IBM computer. *See also* mailing list.

local A word that refers to equipment or processes that are under your direct local control, such as a local host. *Contrast* remote.

log-in A process that enables a user to gain access to a computer system. The log-in procedure typically requires entering a valid username and password in response to computer prompts.

log-off The process to terminate a connection with a computer.

lurking Reading messages on a mailing list or newsgroup without posting any messages. It's good to lurk for awhile when you are new to a group because it helps you determine what the group's unwritten rules are before you start actively participating. It's also important to remember that when you post to a group you do not know who might be lurking.

lurker A noncontributing subscriber.

mail exploder The generic name for programs such as LISTSERV and Majordomo. *See also* LISTSERV, Majordomo, and mailing list.

mailbox The directory on your Internet provider's host computer where your personal mail is stored. When you log on the system, the mail program allows you to access your mail from your mailbox.

mailing list or **maillist** A discussion group operated through a mail exploder. A message sent to the list is sent to everyone who has subscribed to the mailing list. The difference between a mailing list and a newsgroup is that with a mailing list the messages come to your mailbox and with a newsgroup the messages reside on the host computer and you use a software program called a newsreader to look at them. *Contrast* newsgroups.

Majordomo An automatic mailing list distribution system. *See also* mailing list.

menu A list of options a user can select.

mil The domain name that refers to the U.S. military. Probably a U.S. site. *See also* domain.

misc The Usenet newsgroup category that discusses topics that do not fit into the other categories in the hierarchy. *See also* Usenet newsgroups.

moderated Describes a mailing list or newsgroup that has a person who screens the messages, based on criteria established by the group, before the messages are posted. Some people consider this to be censorship, but the quality of the discussion on moderated groups can be higher than that on unmoderated groups because people tend to stay focused on the issues at hand and are not distracted by irrelevant material. Sometimes the term is used to describe a group where messages are not prescreened, but there is a person or persons responsible for keeping the group focused and defusing potentially inflammatory situations.

moderator The person who manages a moderated group.

MUD (Multi-User Dimension) Online fantasy games where the players take on different characters, often in different environments. Players use interactive talk to participate in the game. These adventures are sometimes referred to as virtual reality.

net The domain name that refers to network resources. Probably a U.S. site. *See also* domain.

netiquette Network etiquette.

netism A term that has been created for or has gained a new meaning by its use on the Net. Examples are flame and newbie.

newbie A new user. Also sometimes lovingly referred to as a clueless newbie.

news 1) Short for Usenet newsgroups. 2) The Usenet newsgroup category that discusses news topics. *See also* newsgroups.

newsfeed or **feed** The source of the newsgroups. The newsfeed is downloaded by your provider and stored for a period of time on the host computer. *See also* newsgroups.

newsgroups Discussion groups carried through Usenet. The messages in newsgroups, called articles, are carried in a newsfeed that is downloaded by the system provider and housed on the host computer for a period of time. Newsgroups are set forth in a hierarchy. The first three or four letters of the group define the hierarchy. The eight major news categories are: comp (computer science), news (news network), rec (recreational), sci (scientific research), soc (social issues), talk (topical subjects), misc (miscellaneous groups that do not fit into other categories), and alt (the "anything goes" category).

newsreader The software program that allows you to read and post articles in a newsgroup. The newsreader allows you to select the newsgroup and the articles.

No Carrier The message you receive on your screen if the dial-up connection between your computer and your local host is broken.

node A physical device on a network. *See also* device.

offline 1) Refers to a device that is connected to a computer or a network but cannot respond. 2) The state of not being connected to the Internet. *Contrast* online.

online 1) Refers to a device that is connected to a computer or a network and is able to respond. 2) The state of being connected to the Internet. *Contrast* offline. 3) Something that exists in electronic form, such as an online document.

operators Words or character(s) used in a list of keywords to define the relationships between the keywords. *See also* Boolean search, keywords.

option A choice on a menu.

org The domain that refers to organizations other than the military, government, and educational institutions and commercial organizations. In most cases, this means a nonprofit organization. Probably a U.S. site. *See also* domain.

packet An organized bundle of data that is transported across a network.

page A Web document.

PGP (Pretty Good Privacy) A public domain encryption software.

pointer 1) Another word for a link, pointer originated from the use of the Gopher system. An item on a Gopher menu is called a pointer because when you select it you are "pointing" at a particular item and requesting the Gopher system to "go for" it. *See also* link. 2) A netism used by people when requesting directions for finding something on the Net, as in "Can you give me a pointer to . . . ?"

post 1) (verb) To send a message to a newsgroup or mailing list. 2) (noun) A message posted to a newsgroup or mailing list. *See also* article.

postmaster The administrator of an e-mail site who responds to problems. If you send a message to a site and get an error message in response, you may be able to solicit assistance by sending a message to: postmaster@ (*domain name address*).

PPP (Point-to-Point Protocol) A protocol for transmitting Internet data over serial lines, such as dial-up telephone lines. Both the host and the computer must have PPP installed. PPP does the same thing as SLIP but functions with faster speed and more reliability. *See also* SLIP.

privileges The activities that a user is entitled to engage in on a system. The system administrator assigns privileges to individuals or groups of individuals.

protocol The rules or standards that allow computers to exchange information. *See also* Internet protocol.

provider A company or organization that provides access to the Internet. The service provider may be a government, educational, or nonprofit organization or a commercial company.

public domain Describes a work for which the copyright has expired or to which the copyright owner has disclaimed all rights.

query Posing a question to a database.

queue A waiting area for messages or files or anything else that is sent from one computer to another.

quoting Including text from a message to which you are replying. Quoted material is preceded by a greater-than character (>) in front of each line. Each time a portion of a message is quoted, an additional > character is added. Generally, when you select the reply option from most e-mail programs, the previous message is automatically displayed with the > character. This is an efficient way to engage in a discussion because the issue and response are displayed together. But be sure to edit out any quoted material that is not directly relevant to your response.

readme A file that contains important, useful, and up-to-date information.

real time Occurring at this particular time. Internet Relay Chat conversations, where all of the participants are actually present at their computers, occur in real time. This is not the case with newsgroups or mailing lists. *Contrast* asynchronous.

real world The life and world that still exists when you are offline.

rec The Usenet newsgroup category that discusses topics related to recreation. *See also* newsgroups.

receipt notification A feature of e-mail programs that provides you with a notice when the message you have sent has been placed in the recipient's mailbox.

relevance feedback A method of arranging the feedback from a search request in order of the predicted relevance to the criteria you supplied. The documents are ranked based on the number of times the keywords appeared in them. *See also* keywords.

remote A word that refers to devices or processes that are not under your direct control. If you log on a local host and then Telnet to another computer you are then on a remote host. *Contrast* local.

remote access Using your computer to access a remote computer.

reply A feature of an e-mail program that allows you to respond to a message you have received. The feature automatically takes the information from the header and creates a new header. The new header adds "Re:" in front of the subject. When you reply to a message from a mailing list be sure to check the header carefully so that you don't inadvertently send a message to the list when you intended to send it only to a person, or visa versa.

Request for Discussion A formal proposal to start a new newsgroup.

RFC (Request For Comment) A document that contains Internet protocols, proposed standards, and technical information.

root In systems with hierarchical file systems, the root directory is the directory from which all other directories branch. Similar to a homepage in the Web world.

rot13 Appears in the title of a newsgroup to indicate that the article has been encrypted and contains offensive material.

route The path that data packets take from the point of origination to the destination.

router A device that routes data to the next node on the network.

sci The Usenet newsgroup category that discusses topics related to scientific research. *See also* newsgroups.

search engine Software used to find material on the Internet.

server A specialized device or program that provides service to other devices. Examples are a file server or a mail server. The device or program that makes use of the server is called a client. *See also* client, client/server computing.

shareware A software distribution process where the author of the software makes it freely available, but those who use it are expected to pay the author a fee. *Contrast* freeware, public domain.

SHOUTING WRITING IN ALL CAPS. Considered very rude.

SIG (Special Interest Group) A group of people with a common interest who share messages.

signal-to-noise ratio 1) A measure of the effectiveness of a communication medium. Signal is the quality data; noise is the static that disrupts the data. 2) As used in discussion groups, the measure of quality dialogue to irrelevant material.

signature or **sig** The three to four lines at the bottom of an e-mail message that show your name, address, Internet address, and so on. The e-mail program allows you to create a signature, and then automatically places the signature at the bottom of your message.

site A group of computers that are under a single administrative control.

SLIP (Serial Line Internet Protocol) A protocol for transmitting Internet data over serial lines, such as dial-up telephone lines. *See also* PPP.

smileys Faces that you can type into your messages using the keyboard characters :-). You must look at the figures from a 90-degree angle counterclockwise. Smileys were created to provide a way for users to convey emotions through a text-only system. *See also* emoticons.

snail mail A humorous but slightly derogatory reference to the postal service used by those who have been spoiled by the immediacy of e-mail. Snail mail is still good for shipping chocolate chip cookies, though!

sneakernet When the network goes down, you can always don your sneakers and hand-carry the data on a diskette. This does not work well for cross-country exchanges.

soc The Usenet newsgroup category that discusses topics related to social issues. *See also* newsgroups.

spam or **spamming** Posting an inappropriate and annoying message to a large number of unrelated and uninterested discussion groups. Frequently refers to commercial junk e-mail.

standard disclaimer Language sometimes included in a signature to specify that the speaker is speaking only as a private individual, even though the message originated from an organization, agency, or educational institution. For example, "Opinions contained in this message are those of the author and not the *organization name*." A disclaimer is unlikely to save your neck if you express opinions that could reflect very badly on the organization, agency, or institution.

subscribe To add your name to a mailing list. *Contrast* unsubscribe.

surfing Jumping from host to host or from document to document on the Internet.

system administrator (sysadmin) or **system operator (sysop)** The person who is responsible for the operations of a host computer or a network.

talk 1) A UNIX command that initiates a direct, real-time, back-and-forth written conversation between two users. *See also* chat, Internet Relay Chat. 2) The Usenet newsgroup category that discusses topics related to topical subjects. *See also* newsgroups.

TCP (Transmission Control Protocol) The protocol that ensures data transmission is complete, error-free, and in the proper sequence.

TCP/IP (Transmission Control Protocol/Internet Protocol) The suite of protocols that enable the Internet to function. *See also* TCP, IP.

text file A file that contains only ASCII characters with no special formatting such as boldface or italic. E-mail is transmitted as a text file.

Telnet A program that allows you to login to a remote computer.

terminal or dumb terminal An input-output device that has a keyboard and a video screen but does not have any software or storage area. The terminal is used for communicating with a host computer, which does all of the computing work. Sometimes a personal computer is configured to function as a terminal in relationship to a host; for example, a PC running VT100 connected to an Internet host. *See also* host, terminal/host computing.

terminal/host computing A model for how a dumb terminal interacts with a host computer. The terminal keyboard is used for input, and the screen displays the output, but the host does all of the processing. *Contrast* client/server computing.

thread A series of messages related to the same subject in a discussion group. The thread is identified by the subject listing. With newsreaders, you can have all the messages of the thread presented to you in a coordinated fashion. Some e-mail programs also allow you to sort by subject.

traffic The data flowing through the network.

txt File extension for a text file. *See also* file extension.

Uniform Resource Locator (URL) The specific address for a file that has been placed on the World Wide Web. The URL contains the protocol for accessing the document (http, ftp, etc.), the domain name, and the directory structure through which the document can be located.

unmoderated A discussion group that does not have a moderator. On some unmoderated groups the discussion is free and open. On other unmoderated groups the participants use self-control and sometimes criticism to maintain the focus of the group. *Contrast* moderated.

unsubscribe To remove your name from a mailing list. *Contrast* subscribe.

upload To move data from a local computer to a remote computer. *Contrast* download.

upstream Usenet news flows from one computer to another. The source of the news received by a host computer is considered to be upstream. *Contrast* downstream.

Usenet An electronic bulletin board system. Although Usenet is not part of the Internet, Usenet newsgroups are transmitted over the Internet. *See also* newsgroups.

useraddress *See* e-mail address.

username or **userID** The name under which the user has authorized access to a computer system. Also, the first part of a user address, located to the left of the @ sign.

uu, uud, uue File extensions for a uuencoded file.

uuencode, uudecode Programs that encode and decode files to allow the files to be sent as e-mail.

virtual Not physical; exists in Cyberspace only.

virus A program that can cause damage to software and data on a computer. You should follow virus protection procedures whenever you download a software program from the Internet to avoid spreading a virus.

VT100 A terminal emulation that uses standard communication protocols to allow one computer to communicate with another computer. *See also* terminal.

WAN (Wide Area Network) A long-distance network that connects two or more local area networks (LANs) through dedicated telephone lines or a satellite. *Contrast* LAN.

wasted bandwidth An expression of displeasure over actions that waste bandwidth and try people's patience, such as an irrelevant message or extensive signature.

wildcard A character, such as ? or *, that, when used in a text search, makes it easier to find a match by specifying that any set of characters is appropriate; for example, the keyword "ethic*" will return "ethic", "ethics", or "ethical". *See also* keywords.

World Wide Web (WWW) or **the Web** An Internet information retrieval system that allows you to access material, called Web pages, that have been linked across the Internet by the use of HTML. The Web does not use hierarchical menus. The linking capability forms what is, in essence, a Web of information.

Web page An individual file accessed through the Web. A Web page is constructed using HTML and contains links to other Web pages or to other locations within the particular Web page. *See also* HTML, World Wide Web.

worm A computer program that infests a network environment and copies itself repeatedly. *See also* virus.

WYSIWYG What You See Is What You Get. Meaning that what you see on your screen is what will be printed.

Net Communication Conventions

Bold and Italics

Because e-mail is transmitted in ASCII form, material cannot be printed or displayed in bold, italicized, or underlined formats. Therefore, the following conventions have been established:

✦ The asterisk (*) is considered the equivalent of boldfaced type. A *special* emphasis can be given to a word or phrase when it is *really* important.

✦ The underline (_) is used in messages to denote words that should be italicized or underlined, and is generally used for the names of publications. In an e-mail message this book would be referred to as _The Cyberethics Reader_.

Smileys

The following are some common and fun smileys that have been created to add a bit of character to an e-mail message:

:-)	basic smile
;-)	winking smile
:-/	undecided
:-0	shocked
:-(	sad
:-&	tongue-tied
8-)	glasses and a smile
8-#	dead
%-)	cross-eyed
:-x	my lips are sealed
:-p	sticking out tongue
{:-)	smile with beret
:-)8	snazzy dresser
*:o)	Bozo the clown
8-0	what next!
#:-)	smile with straight hair
$:-)	Smile with curly hair
8-0[=[]	The author's personal creation—me on a soapbox

TLAs (Three-Letter Acronyms)

Some places on the Net make frequent use of three (more or less) letter acronyms. These are some of the most common:

BCNU	Be seein' you
BFN	Bye for now
BTW	By the way
FWIW	For what it's worth
FYI	For your information
GD&R	Grinning, ducking, and running (usually in response to a sarcastic comment made in jest)
IANAL or IANAD	I am not a lawyer or I am not a doctor
IMCO	In my considered opinion
IMHO	In my humble opinion (often used by someone who is actually not being humble)
IMNSHO	In my not-so-humble opinion
IMO	In my opinion
LL&P	Live long and prosper
LOL	Laughing out loud
MOTD	Message of the day
OIC	Oh, I see.
OTF	On the floor
OTFL	On the floor laughing
OTOH	On the other hand
ROTFL	Rolling on the floor laughing
RSN	Real soon now (but probably not)
RTFM	Read the _____ manual (used in response to people who ask dumb questions)
TLA	Three-letter acronym
TTFN	Ta-ta for now
WRT	With respect to
YMMV	Your mileage may vary (translation: your experience may differ)
YR	Yeah, right

Index

Just because you can, doesn't make it right
Those are real people out there
Speak responsibly
Look your best
Respect the privacy of others
Remain cool under fire
We all begin as clueless newbies
Tread carefully
Play by the rules of the house
Don't make noise
Respect resource limits
Ensure the integrity of the system
Don't go where you don't belong
Don't pollute
Watch where you are looking
When someone tells you to stop, stop
If it's not true, don't say it
Don't take candy from strangers
Read between the lines
If it seems too good to be true, it probably is
Credit the source
Don't take without permission
Speak up for your rights
Get a life
Expand your mind
Read with your eyes open
Share your expertise
Lend a helping hand
Feel the funk, but do it anyway
We are one world

(Tear off or copy this page and post it in a prominent place.)